THE
TITANIC

igloo

igloo

Published in 2011
by Igloo Books Ltd
Cottage Farm
Sywell
NN6 0BJ

www.igloo-books.com

B044 1111
2 4 6 8 10 9 7 5 3 1
ISBN 978-0-85780-251-4

Images supplied courtesy of
Getty Images, 101 Bayham Steet, London, NW1 0AG

Written By
Michael Swift

Distributed in association with G2 Entertainment Limited
Printed and manufactured in China

Contents

Introduction

It is now almost 100 years since the supposedly unsinkable White Star liner Titanic sank beneath the waves and into the history books. In the years that followed that night to remember in April 1912 much has been written about the ship and the tragic loss of life that occurred following its collision with an iceberg during its maiden voyage to New York, but still the Titanic continues to fascinate. In film, too, the story of the sinking has been told or reinterpreted on several occasions – from *A Night to Remember,* based on Walter Lord's pioneering history of the sinking, through *Raise the Titanic,* Sir

Lew Grade's costly film about an attempted salvage operation (he was alleged to have stated after the making of the film that it would have been cheaper to have lowered the Atlantic), and, most recently James Cameron's blockbuster *Titanic* starring Kate Winslet and Leonardo di Caprio. With the discovery of the wreck, a whole new industry has been spawned with film crews recording the ship's remains and tours down to view it. Artefacts have been removed from the debris field and concern over the wreck's condition has led to legal action over its actual ownership. For more than 70 years the wreck of the *Titanic*

LEFT
A scene from the film *A Night to Remember.*

lay undisturbed; such has been the activity over the past 20 years since it was discovered that its condition has deteriorated rapidly and the wreck may well completely disintegrate by the end of the current century.

The fascination with the sinking of the *Titanic* is easy to explain. The loss of such a prestigious ship on its maiden voyage was bound to cause interest, particularly as the passenger list included many of the era's rich and famous, leading to rumours that the ship was conveying a veritable treasure trove of these individuals' wealth. There was the drama of the actual sinking itself, with stories of

heroism and human frailties; the band playing on as the ship slid under the waves alongside the failure of the crew to utilise to the full the admittedly inadequate lifeboat provision. There were tales of individual heroism, such as Thomas Andrew's, the shipbuilder's manager, endeavouring to warn as many passengers as possible before accepting his own fate and of those employed in the wireless room who stuck to their posts as long as possible in trying to summon assistance to the stricken vessel. This book is designed to provide an overview of the history of the sinking of the *Titanic* and of its aftermath.

Chapter One

White Star Line

Although popularly known as White Star Line, the company's correct name was the Oceanic Steam Navigation Company when it was created by Thomas Ismay in the late 1860s. However, the roots of the business stretched back to earlier in the century.

The original White Star Line, founded in Liverpool by John Pilkington and Henry Threlfall Wilson, was designed to capitalise upon trade with Australia, following the discovery of gold. Initially it operated chartered sailing ships, but was to acquire its first steamship, the Royal Standard, in 1863. Following a merger with two other shipping lines – the Black Ball and Eagle – the company became the Liverpool, Melbourne & Oriental Steam Navigation Co Ltd. However, this new business was not successful, and White Star separated to concentrate on the increasingly lucrative transatlantic business. With the expansion westwards of the United States of America and the potential opportunities that the growing US economy offered, vast numbers of European migrants were encouraged to leave hardships at home to seek fame and future across the Atlantic and, for the shipping companies, this represented a potentially lucrative business. For the newly separated White Star Line, however, whilst the business may have held promise, its finances did not. Heavily in debt to the Royal Bank of Liverpool, to the tune of £527,000, the failure of the bank in October 1867 forced the relatively new shipping line into bankruptcy.

However, one man's business failure is another's opportunity and, in January 1868, Thomas Ismay, a director of the National Line, paid the princely sum of £1,000 to acquire the trade name, flag and goodwill of the White Star Line. However, the new business, to be based at Albion House in Liverpool, required new finance and, to achieve this, Ismay entered into an agreement with Gustav Schwabe, a German financier who was already heavily involved with the Belfast-based shipbuilders Harland & Wolff. Schwabe guaranteed the funding of the purchase provided that Ismay placed orders for any vessels with Harland & Wolff. This was agreed and, on 30 July 1869, the first orders were placed. The order was for four vessels: the Oceanic, Atlantic, Baltic and Republic. Whilst work was underway on the construction of the first new ships, Ismay created the Oceanic Steam Navigation Company to operate them; the new company, with a capital of £400,000 in £1,000 shares, was formed on 6 September 1869.

Following the completion of the line's first vessels, services between Liverpool and New York via Queenstown – as Cobh in Ireland was then called – commenced in 1871 but disaster was soon to strike. On 20 March

RIGHT
Shipowner Thomas
Henry Ismay, the
founder of the White
Star Line.

1873, the line's second steamship, the Atlantic (which had undertaken her maiden voyage on 6 June 1871), set sail from Liverpool on her nineteenth transatlantic crossing. It was destined to be her last. Adverse weather conditions meant that the ship made slow progress on her journey towards New York with the result that, by 31 March, the ship was still 460 miles east of Sandy Hook, the entrance to New York harbour, but with only 128 tons of coal on board. This was insufficient to get the ship to New York as it was estimated that this was sufficient for only some 380 miles. The ship's captain, James Agnew Williams, decided therefore to head for Halifax, Nova Scotia, which was only some 170 miles away. Shortly before

midnight on the 31st, Williams retired to bed, giving instructions to the watch on the bridge that, if ice was seen or if visibility deteriorated, he was to be raised immediately. However, his instructions both about this and being raised under any circumstances at 3am were ignored or forgotten and, around 3.15am on 1 April 1873, the ship struck rocks off Meagher's Island, Newfoundland. As with the Titanic 41 years later, the Atlantic had been fitted with insufficient lifeboat capacity to remove safely all the passengers and crew – although the numbers provided did exceed by some 50% the actual Board of Trade regulations in force at the time – and of

MAIN
The Oceanic of the White Star Line was the largest liner in the world when she was launched in 1899.

those on board, the lifeboats on the port side were smashed before they could be used by the force of the sea and, on the starboard side, suffered severely as well, with No 5 with more than 40 crew and passengers on board, for example, being crushed as the ship listed more severely. In all, out of the 966 on board, some 565 men, women and children all died. At the time this was the greatest maritime disaster in history. Captain Williams, who survived, was held partially to blame by the subsequent inquiry held into the disaster.

Despite the loss of the Atlantic, White Star Line's fortunes continued and in 1878 the then head of Cunard, John Burns, proposed that the two companies should merge. This proposal was declined as White Star Line continued to develop its own fleet. On 26 March 1883, the line took delivery of its first steel ship – the Ionic; this, and her sister ship the Doric, were the first to be fitted with engines actually constructed by Harland & Wolff itself.

For the next 20 years, White Star Line maintained its independent existence but, behind the scenes, the noted financier John Pierpoint Morgan was endeavouring to construct a

cartel that could dominate the transatlantic trade and ensure higher prices through less competition. In 1902, Morgan created, from his existing interests, the International Mercantile Marine Company, increasing at the same time the business's capital from $15 million to $120 million. Using the money raised, Morgan bought into a number of shipping lines, including Atlantic Transport, Leyland and Dominion, and was also interested in acquiring Cunard. This latter deal was thwarted by the British government offering a soft loan to Cunard, which allowed the line to construct the Lusitania and Mauretania, whilst also providing £150,000 per annum as part of the mail contract. The German-owned Hamburg-Amerika and North German Lloyd lines were also targeted, but rejected Morgan's advances. After a bitter battle in which William Pirrie of Harland & Wolff backed Morgan rather than J Bruce Ismay, White Star Line was acquired by IMM for £10 million.

The newly enlarged IMM cartel was not strong financially as it had not been able to eliminate all the competition as Morgan had hoped and, by 1903, Morgan realised that he needed an experienced operator to run the

ABOVE
The transatlantic liner SS Mauretania

business. He approached Ismay, who initially declined Morgan's offer, but, in February 1904, a deal was finally struck and Ismay became chairman and managing director of IMM. The scene was set for the development and construction of the 'Olympic' class of liner in order to compete with the new ships under construction for Cunard, both of which entered service in 1906.

Cunard's new liners had been built for speed, an effort to wrest the 'Blue Riband' title for the fastest crossing of the north Atlantic, but there was a price to be paid for speed. Each additional knot required ever increasing amounts of coal and this added both to weight and cost. In looking towards Olympic and her sister vessels, White Star Line decided against competing on speed but in favour of providing the greater luxury.

Thus, the Titanic was designed for a cruising speed of 21 knots with a maximum of 23.75 knots whilst the Mauretania achieved a maximum of 27 knots.

The construction of the three great liners with which the White Star Line will forever be associated commenced with the laying down of the keel of Olympic – yard No 400 – in 1908. Of the three, only one ever completed a commercial sailing, with Titanic being sunk on her maiden voyage and Britannic, converted for use as a hospital ship, sinking in the Aegean Sea before she could enter commercial service, following a mine strike during World War 1. The basic design for the three ships was agreed by J Bruce Ismay following a trip to Belfast on 29 July 1908; having approved the basic concept, Ismay signed the first Letter of Agreement

LEFT
Olympic in the
Harland and Wolff
yard prior to launch.

covering the construction two days later. Curiously, the three Letters of Agreement signed for the three 'Olympic' class ships – one for each of the three constructed – represented the only contracts ever concluded between White Star Line and Harland & Wolff, despite the vast amount of work undertaken by the latter on behalf of the former.

White Star Line continued to provide transatlantic services after the Titanic disaster. However, trading conditions in the period after 1920, particularly after the Wall Street Crash of 1929 and the start of the Great Depression, resulted in the deterioration of the company's finances. White Star Line was not unique; Cunard as well was financially weak and had been forced to suspend work on the construction of its new liner, the future Queen Mary, in Belfast. In 1933, the British government agreed to provide financial

assistance to the two lines provided that they merge and an agreement for this merger was concluded on 30 December 1933 with the actual merger being completed on 10 May 1934. The new fleet comprised 10 ships from White Star Line, including the increasingly aged Olympic, and 15 from Cunard (with the sixteenth, the future Queen Mary, under construction). As a result, the new company – Cunard-White Star Limited – was owned 62% by the shareholders of Cunard and 38% by the shareholders of White Star Line. In 1947, Cunard bought out the 38% it didn't own and, on 31 December 1949, the name reverted to Cunard alone. By 1950, only two of the ex-White Star Line ships, the Georgic and Britannic, remained in service; these were the last ships to carry the White Star burgee (flag) of a broad red pennant with two tails and a white pointed star above that of Cunard.

Chapter Two

Harland & Wolff Shipbuilders

The famous Belfast shipbuilding yard of Harland & Wolff, situated on Queen's Island, was established in 1861 by Edward James Harland (1831–1895) and by Gustav Wilhelm Wolff (1834–1913). Harland had been employed as General Manager of the yard since 1858 by the yard's then owner Robert Hickson. Wolff, born in Hamburg, Germany, was the nephew of the financier Gustav Schwabe. Wolff moved to Belfast in

1848 where his German connections came in useful when the new business was set up, as Schwabe was a major investor in the Bibby shipping line and it was from the Bibby Line that Harland & Wolff received its first orders for three 270-foot long steamships.

One of the factors that helped Harland & Wolff succeed in the shipbuilding business was in altering the designs of ships. Innovations that the yard developed included the use of iron for upper decks rather than wood, which increased the strength of the vessels, and adopting a squarer but flatter section for the hulls, which increased each individual ship's capacity.

In the period of some 50 years leading up to 1925, the Harland & Wolff shipyard was perhaps the greatest in the world; this was, however, not to lead to vast profits as the increasingly competitive nature of transatlantic shipping drove the yard's customers to seek ever more competitive prices for the construction of their new vessels. One of these customers was the newly-established White Star Line.

The common factor between White Star and Harland & Wolff was Gustav Schwabe; he was a shareholder in the shipyard and was also one of the early backers of White Star Line. His involvement in the latter was on condition that White Star Line acquire its vessels from Harland & Wolff on the basis of cost price plus 4%. The first White Star Line vessel built in Belfast, the Oceanic, was launched on 27 August 1870 at a cost of £120,000; she was quickly followed by five further vessels – the Atlantic, Baltic, Republic, Adriatic and Celtic. In all, Harland & Wolff would construct 75 vessels for White Star Line, including the three 'Olympic' class liners, between then and the late 1920s.

The rationale for the construction of the class in 1907 was a desire on the part of J Bruce Ismay, managing director of White Star Line, to construct a class of steamship that would give his company a competitive edge over the Cunard Line's RMS Lusitania and RMS Mauretania.

In 1894, on the death of James Harland, William James Pirrie became the company's chairman, a post he was to fill until his own death in 1924. Harland & Wolff survived the tragedy to remain a major employer in the Belfast area and, although the company's last actual construction was of the MV Anvil Point in 2003, the yard remains active with ship repair and conversion work and in other areas of engineering. The Belfast skyline remains dominated by the two massive cranes – Samson (built in 1974) and Goliath (1969) – that still stand sentinel over the works.

MAIN
Samson and Goliath
Harland & Wolff's
famous cranes as
seen today.

Chapter Three

The Sister Ships

There were to be three 'Olympic' class liners built by Harland & Wolff; Titanic was the second completed. The decision to construct the three vessels was made between J Bruce Ismay, chairman of White Star Line, William Pirrie, the Chairman of Harland & Wolff, and Thomas Andrews, head of the shipyard's draughting department and managing director. The intention was to construct a series of steamships that would surpass in luxury the recently constructed RMS Lusitania and RMS Mauretania, built for the rival transatlantic line Cunard.

The first of the trio to be laid down, on 16 December 1908, was the Olympic but before work could commence, the yard itself had to be modified in order to accommodate

LEFT
Captain of the Olympic John Smith (right) with William James Pirrie, chairman of Harland & Wolff.

the vast size of the planned ships. This work included the conversion of the Belfast yard's three slipways into two. Also constructed was a huge gantry over the rebuilt slipways; built feet high. The Olympic was launched on 20 October 1910 and, as completed, was 882 feet 3 inches in length with a beam of 92 feet 6 inches. Her tonnage as built was 45,324 (although this was increased to 46,439 after 1912 and the fitting of additional lifeboats, giving her a displacement of 52,067 tons). Her planned service speed was 21 knots with a maximum speed of 23.75 knots. Following fitting out, the Olympic's maiden voyage started on 14 June 1911. As was usual, White Star Line's commodore – Captain Edward Smith – was the ship's captain and a party from Harland & Wolff, led by Thomas Andrews, was also on board for the trip to New York.

The Olympic's maiden voyage progressed smoothly until she approached New York harbour on 21 June 1911; with the presence of the harbour pilot and the assistance of 12 tugs, the Olympic was being carefully guided towards Pier 59. Unfortunately, one of the tugs was dragged by the backwash from one of the liner's massive propellers and was temporarily crushed under the liner's stern. Fortunately, however, there were no casualties, but it did mark the start of a series of incidents that marred the early career of the Olympic and led to her being returned to Belfast on two occasions for repairs, which led to delays in the completion of her sister ship, Titanic.

The most critical of these incidents was the collision with HMS Hawke on 20 September 1911. This occurred when the Olympic was departing from Southampton on her fifth transatlantic crossing. The exit from Southampton harbour was and

remains a difficult one for large vessels and, as usual, the Olympic had on board a pilot, the experienced Captain William George Bowyer, who would guide the liner as far out as the Nab Lightship. As the Olympic undertook the tricky manoeuvre to pass through towards the English Channel via the Spithead route, a Royal Navy armoured cruiser, HMS Hawke commanded by Commander William Frederick Blunt, was returning to the naval base at Portsmouth following sea trials. HMS Hawke was an elderly vessel, one of six members of the 'Edgar' class of cruiser, weighing some 7,350 tons and having been built originally in the late 1880s. Out of date by the early years of the 20th century, HMS Hawke could still achieve its maximum speed of 19.5 knots. More critical, however, was the bow design

of warships of the late 19th century; unlike modern warships, where the bow curves up from the sea in the case of those constructed earlier, the bow curved into the sea as it was believed that the bow could be used to ram enemy ships if the opportunity presented itself. How potent such an armoured ram could be was demonstrated to good effect on 20 September 1911 when, as both ships failed to take adequate avoiding action, the Hawke rammed the White Star liner some 86 feet from her stern.

The damage to the Olympic comprised a vertical gash, some eight feet in depth, that extended from D deck as far down as G deck and thus below the waterline. With the watertight doors being closed on both vessels, there was no danger that the Olympic would sink but water did penetrate. In addition, one of the ship's propellers was also damaged. As a result of tidal conditions, Olympic dropped its anchor and so did not return to Southampton harbour until the following day. Following inspection by Harland & Wolff staff in the company's repair facility, it was decided that the damage was too extensive to be repaired in Southampton and that Olympic would need to return to Belfast for repair. Temporary patches were fitted over the damaged section and, with a skeleton crew on board, Olympic set sail for Belfast on 4 October 1911. Repairs to the Olympic took some six weeks to complete, costing White Star Line some £250,000

in lost revenue and repair bills. On 20 November, Olympic departed for her much delayed fifth transatlantic crossing. Not only had the White Star Line lost out heavily in terms of lost revenue and repair costs, but the company was also blamed in the report of the Royal Navy Court of Enquiry. The decision was hotly contested by White Star Line and the ultimate liability was ultimately determined through a prolonged court case, which was not settled until 9 November 1914 when the House of Lords finally passed judgement. By that date, of course, a number of major players in the accident, including Captain Smith (on board the Titanic when it sank) and HMS Hawke

MAIN
The Olympic was the first of her class, built for White Star Line.

(sunk by a German U-boat in mid-October 1914), were no longer concerned.

The next incident to affect the Olympic occurred during her fourth return trip from New York following repair. Striking a submerged obstacle, believed to be a wreck, a blade from one of Olympic's propellers was destroyed; although not unique, this loss for Olympic was significant in that it required a further trip to Belfast for repair, as the Harland & Wolff shipyard was the only yard with a dry-dock capable of accommodating the ship. Following the Olympic's return to Southampton at the end of this voyage, she sailed once more to Belfast, arriving at the yard on 1 March 1912 for repair. Following repair, the Olympic was again put into service and she was at sea at the time of the sinking of the Titanic, albeit too far from her sister ship to offer assistance.

Following the sinking of the Titanic, action was taken immediately to increase the number of collapsible lifeboats on board but the crew refused to serve on board the vessel again unless more regular lifeboats were installed. White Star Line agreed. Later in 1912, the ship was again returned to Belfast, this time for further modification. The work included the raising of the internal bulkheads and the installation of a second hull. Following this work, the Olympic re-entered service in early 1913.

On the outbreak of World War 1, the Olympic initially continued in commercial use, although she did rescue the crew from HMS Audacious on 27 October 1914 when the warship had been seriously damaged by enemy action; an attempt, however, to tow the stricken warship failed when the tow ropes broke. In September 1915, however, the Olympic was requisitioned for use as a troopship. Repainted in camouflage markings and fitted with guns, Olympic, now re-designated as His Majesty's Transport No 2810, was first used to ship men to the Gallipoli campaign on 24 September 1915 when she departed from Liverpool. She was to serve in the

eastern Mediterranean until transferred in 1916 for use in shipping Canadian soldiers across the Atlantic and, after the USA declared war in 1917, she performed a similar function for US troops. As a transport ship she was a recognised military target and, on 12 May 1918, she survived a torpedo attack launched by German submarine U-103. Turning the tables on the Germans, the Olympic's captain, Bertram Fox-Hayes, ordered the Olympic to ram the submarine, resulting in the only known case of a merchant vessel sinking a U-boat during World War 1.

After the cessation of hostilities, the Olympic returned once more to Belfast where she was refitted for a return to civilian use, returning to service in 1920. During the 1920s she remained in service, seeing

modifications during the period as her configuration was changed to meet the changing passenger market. She underwent her final refit in 1933 before suffering the indignity of one final collision when, on 15 May 1934, she hit the Nantucket Lightship, causing the smaller vessel to sink with the loss of seven member of the 11-man crew.

In 1934, following pressure from the British government, White Star and Cunard merged and the new company started to rationalise its fleet, targeting the older White Star ships – of which Olympic was one – first. Nicknamed by this date 'Old Reliable', Olympic was taken out of service during 1935. After partial scrapping at Jarrow, the Olympic's hull was towed to the famous scrap yard at Inverkeithing, just north of Edinburgh where the dismantling

was completed in 1937. Prior to scrapping, fixtures and fittings from the Olympic were auctioned off.

The third of the class was originally to be named Gigantic, but this was changed to Britannic following the sinking of the Titanic. The Britannic was laid down on 30 November 1911 and was launched on 26 February 1914. She was the largest of the three ships built, with a length of 882 feet nine inches and beam of 94 feet. Her tonnage was 58,158 gross tonnes giving a displacement of 53,000 tons. Fitted with 29 boilers and with three engines driving three propellers, the Britannic was capable of a maximum speed of 23.75 knots.

However, before Britannic could be completed, in August 1914 Britain declared war on Germany and World War 1 engulfed Europe. Immediately on the declaration

of war, priority in shipyards was diverted towards the completion of naval work and work on the Britannic was much delayed. It was not until May 1915 that Britannic completed mooring trials of her engines. By this date, however, the Admiralty had started requisitioning large liners to act as either troop or hospital ships for the campaign in Gallipoli. On 13 November 1915 Britannic was requisitioned as HMHS Britannic and she entered service as a hospital ship under the command of Captain Charles A Bartlett. As a hospital ship she was repainted white with prominent red crosses and green stripe. Between November 1915 and November 1916, HMHS Britannic completed safely five round trips to Gallipoli and back to the UK. However, on 12 November 1916, she set sail on her sixth, and final, voyage to the Greek island of Lemnos.

Passing Gibraltar on 15 November and refuelling at Naples on 17 November, HMHS Britannic departed from Naples on 18 November before passing through the Strait of Messina. Cape Matapan was passed on 21 November and, later that morning, the ship was sailing at full speed – 21 knots – into the Kea Channel, between Cape Sounion and the island of Kea. At 8.12am a loud explosion was heard, shaking the ship. Captain Bartlett, on the bridge with Chief Officer Hume, was soon aware of the seriousness of the position. The explosion – cause uncertain at the time but now known to have been the result of striking a mine – had hit the ship's starboard side between holds two and three and had resulted in the bulkheads between hold one and the forepeak also being damaged. This meant that the sea was flooding into four of the watertight compartments. This was compounded by damage to the firemen's tunnel leading from their quarters to boiler room six with the result that water was also entering the boiler room.

Following the loss of the Titanic, the design of the Britannic had been modified so that she would remain afloat if the first six watertight compartments were flooded and she was motionless; unlike the Titanic, where the bulkheads only extended to E deck, on Britannic these had been raised up to B deck. However, although Bartlett ordered the closing of all the watertight doors, the explosion seems to have caused some distortion with the result that the watertight door between boiler rooms five and six could not be closed, resulting in water entering boiler room five. This, however, should not have caused the ship to sink but the survivability of the ship had been further compromised by the opening of portholes earlier in order to ventilate the wards. As the ship listed so water started to enter the vessel through these openings and, from this point, the ship was doomed. Indeed, despite the modifications undertaken after the 1912 disaster, the Britannic was actually sinking more rapidly than its sister. In order to try to save the ship, Bartlett decided to try and run aground on the island of Kea, some three miles away to the south, although with the ship's list a sharp turn to starboard was not an easy manoeuvre.

Captain Bartlett's plans, however, came into conflict with actions being taken elsewhere on the stricken ship. There was some confusion over the lifeboats, where, on the one hand, Assistant Commander Harry William Dyke was endeavouring to organise the ordered launching of the lifeboats from the aft davits on the starboard deck, whilst other crew members, in panic, were taking their own action. At about 8.30, two lifeboats were launched without authorisation; these dropped six feet into the water and were almost immediately smashed by the giant propellers causing both lifeboats and their occupants to be cut to ribbons.

Made aware both of the loss from this incident and of the fact that the speed of the vessel was causing more rapid flooding, Captain Bartlett decided to stop the engines. This action saved a third lifeboat, full of men from the Royal Army Medical Corps, from suffering the same fate as the earlier two. At 8.35 Bartlett gave the command to abandon ship although the ship's increasing list made use of davits almost impossible after about 8.45. At 09.00 Captain Bartlett, who had

MAIN
The launch of White Star Liner Britannic from Belfast. The sister ship of Olympic and Titanic. She sank in the Aegean Sea in November 1916.

remained on the bridge, ordered one final blast on the whistle; this was the signal for the ship's engineers, commanded by Chief Engineer Robert Fleming, to make good their escape via the staircase into funnel No 4. Bartlett himself abandoned ship, swimming to one of the collapsible lifeboats.

As the Britannic continued to list further towards its starboard side, the funnels collapsed and equipment from the ship fell overboard. Finally, as the ship's stern rose into the air, the Britannic finally sank at 09.07. Of those on board, the first were rescued by Greek fishermen from the adjacent island of Kea, before two Royal Navy warships – HMS Scourge and HMS Heroic – arrived to assist in the picking up of survivors. These ships, already fully loaded with survivors, were joined by a third, HMS Foxhound, later in the morning and by a fourth, HMS Foresight, early in the

afternoon. Of those on board the Britannic, a total of 1,036 were saved with only 30 losing their lives. It was fortunate that the ship was heading outbound to the war zone; if it had been on the return journey, laden with wounded soldiers then, undoubtedly, the loss of life would have been much greater.

Following the sinking, the wreck of the Britannic sat in some 120m of water in the Aegean Sea off the island of Kea. It was first discovered by the noted French marine biologist and explorer Jacques Cousteau in 1975 and his survey showed well the impact of the mine and the damage sustained as the ship sank. More recently, in 1996, Dr Robert Ballard and, in 2003, Carl Spencer, have both undertaken further exploration of the wreck side. These investigations have shone more light onto the loss of the Britannic, confirming, for example, the presence of mine anchors and so settling the debate about whether the ship had struck a mine or been torpedoed by one of the German submarines known to have been operating in the area.

Chapter Four

Building The Titanic

Work was not yet complete on the Olympic when the Titanic was laid down on 31 March 1909 at yard No 401 with hull No 390904. The second in the 'Olympic' class was to be 882 feet nine inches in length, making her six inches longer than the Olympic, but with an identical beam of 92 feet six inches and with a draught of 34 feet seven inches. The Titanic had a Gross Registered Tonnage of 46,238 and a displacement of 52,310 tons. She was fitted with two reciprocating four-cylinder, triple expansion steam engines, for the side propellers, and a single low-pressure Parsons turbine, for the central propeller. The engines, which powered the three propellers (two bronze triple-blade side propellers and one bronze four-blade central propeller), were fed by 25 double-ended and four single-ended Scotch-type boilers, rated at 215psi, fired by 159 coal-burning furnaces. In all, the engines provided enough power to achieve a maximum speed of 23.75 knots with a service speed of 21 knots.

The ship was constructed with a double hull, designed to accommodate water for use in the boilers and additional water to provide ballast (and thus stability) whilst at sea. The ship was, however, designed and built with only a single-skin hull. One of the lessons of the sinking was that, in future, ships were constructed with double skin hulls. The class was designed with four funnels; of these, three were used to exhaust the engine room, whilst the fourth was designed to ventilate the engine rooms and provide the air required to keep the fires in the furnaces alight. Thus steam and smoke should only ever have been seen emerging from the leading three funnels; images that show smoke emerging from the fourth are incorrect. As a further gesture towards safety, the Olympic and Titanic were also fitted with watertight compartments separated by strong bulkheads; in the case of the latter, there were 16 compartments. These were divided by doors held up in the open position by electro-magnetic latches; in the event of an emergency, the doors could, theoretically, be closed rapidly by use of a switch on the bridge. Unfortunately, whilst these transverse bulkheads offered considerable protection, their failure to extend through the full height of the ship – they extended only to 10 feet above the water line – meant that, once a number of compartments were compromised, water could seep over the top. Following the loss of the Titanic, the third vessel in the class, the Britannic, had her design modified to reduce this risk.

RIGHT
Titanic in construction in the Arrol Gantry at the Harland & Wolff shipyard, Belfast.

Chapter Four

The Titanic was designed to carry 3,547 in total (2,603 passengers with a crew of 944). On the maiden voyage, a total of 1,317 passengers were on board, comprising 324 first class, 285 second class and 708 third class as well as 891 members of crew. In case of emergency, the Titanic was fitted with 20 lifeboats; although this was more than required legally (under regulations introduced in 1894, a ship of 10,000 tons or more only need to carry 16 lifeboats) those on board the Titanic had a capacity of 980 in total; the four additional Englehardt collapsibles provided an additional 196. The Titanic was, therefore, provided with accommodation in its lifeboats for about a third of the total number of passengers and crew on board if she were fully loaded; however, the growth in the size of ships since then made the regulation patently inadequate and the Titanic was provided with lifeboat accommodation for barely half its passengers and crew despite having four additional collapsibles (over the maximum required), it was still inadequate in the event of an emergency. But then, of course, no-one expected the Titanic to face such an eventuality – in the words of the eminent contemporary trade publication *The Shipbuilder*, the Titanic was 'practically unsinkable'.

It has been suggested that one reason for the ship's fate was the quality of steel used in its construction. Following recovery of a part of the ship's hull, the steel used was subjected to detailed analysis. The tests

MAIN
Titanic in dry dock, February 1912.

showed that at low temperatures – and at the point the Titanic struck the iceberg the water temperature was 31°F – the steel would become weaker and prone to 'brittle fracture' as a result of the higher level of sulphur in the metal. The report concluded that the real tragedy of the Titanic was that better construction techniques and a better quality of steel plate might have averted her loss or resulted in an even slower rate of flooding that may have saved more crew and passengers. The reality, however, was that the builders of the ship used the best quality steel available to them at the time and, whilst perhaps not up to modern standards of construction and thickness, the robustness of the hull is amply demonstrated by how well it withstood hitting the sea bed. Ultimately, the fate of the ship wasn't determined by the thickness or quality of the steel plating used but by the inherent weakness of its design in terms of the lack of full bulkheads.

Although the Titanic was already provided with more than the legal requirement for lifeboats, the ship's designers had allowed for the installation of a total of 64 in case the Board of Trade regulation changed during the ship's construction. It was alleged at the US Inquiry – but refuted by Harold Sanderson, the vice-president of International Mercantile Marine – the decision not to install the additional lifeboats had been made at the insistence of Ismay who feared that the additional davits and lifeboats would have reduced the passenger promenade area on the boat deck.

BELOW
The massive anchor of Titanic is transported to its destination by horsedrawn cart.

There were moreover a couple of features within the actual design of the ship that were potential weaknesses. Of these the most significant was the ship's triple-screw configuration. The two outermost propellers were powered by reciprocating steam engines, which were reversible; the central screw was driven by a steam turbine, which was not reversible. This meant that when First Officer Murdoch issued orders to reverse

engines in order to avoid hitting the iceberg, he actually undermined the manoeuvrability of the vessel as the central turbine could not reverse during the 'full steam astern' order and so simply stopped turning. In addition, the location of the central propeller directly in front of the rudder resulted in the diminution of the rudder's effectiveness. The training procedures for the 'Olympic' class ships laid down that the correct method for dealing with the problem faced by Murdoch would have been to switch the port propeller to full astern whilst retaining full steam ahead with the remaining two engines. This would have had the effect of making the ship turn sharply to port and thus, theoretically, pulling away from the iceberg. It's impossible to tell whether, had Murdoch adopted the correct method, the ship would have avoided the iceberg; conventional wisdom, however, suggests that the speed and proximity of the Titanic were such that the collision was inevitable.

The problem with the propellers compounded the design of the rudder itself. Whilst, as with the lifeboats, the provision was within the legal limits, the rudder was too small for a ship the size of the Titanic. Although the rudders fitted to the contemporary Cunard liners Mauretania and Lusitania were much bigger than that fitted to either the Olympic or Titanic, worries over the increasing size of ships and of manoeuvring them in an emergency were not major priorities as far as White Star and Harland & Wolff were concerned.

Following the laying down of the keel, which started on 21 March 1909, work proceeded on ship No 401 rapidly with the ship being launched on 31 May 1911. Amongst the guests at the launch was the American financier John Pierpoint Morgan;

he was one of an estimated crowd of some 100,000 that witnessed the launch shortly after noon. On top of the gantry above the ship flew the Union Flag on one side with the Stars & Stripes on the other, with the White Star Line's red pennant flying in the middle. Below, a line of signal flags proclaimed the message 'SUCCESS'. Later the same day, at around 4.30pm, Titanic's sister ship, the Olympic, sailed from Belfast for Liverpool with both J Bruce Ismay and John Pierpoint Morgan onboard. Simultaneously, the two tenders designed for use at Cherbourg – the Nomadic and the Traffic – headed southwards towards the French port. With the Olympic now completed, the Harland & Wolff yard could turn its attention towards the final completion of the Titanic with a view to the ship's maiden voyage occurring on 20 March 1912.

However, fitting out of the ship was delayed by the two incidents to the Olympic – the collision with HMS Hawke and the loss of a propeller – which both required the older ship to return to Belfast for repair. On the occasion of the first return, it became evident that the work involved would

cause serious delays to the completion of the Titanic and, on 10 October 1911, it was announced that the new ship's maiden voyage would now be Wednesday 10 April 1912. The resultant delays meant that it was not until 10am on Tuesday 2 April 1912 that the Titanic was ready to start her sea trials. On board were 78 members of the 'black gang' – those required to work the engines – and 41 officers and senior crew, including Captain Edward Smith who boarded his new command for the first time on 1 April. Although J Bruce Ismay could not attend as a result of family matters, White Star Line was

MAIN
Titanic being guided down Belfast Lough by the tugs Hercules, Huskisson, Herculaneum and Hornby.

represented by Harold Sanderson, one of the company's directors. Lord Pirrie was another absentee; he could not be on board as a result of illness, but Thomas Andrews was on board, representing Harland & Wolff as was Edward Wilding, a marine architect. Assisted by tugs (the Hornby on the starboard line; the Herald out in front and the Herculaneum and Huskisson on the starboard and port lines), the Titanic slipped its moorings and entered the Victoria Channel towards Belfast Lough at around 6.00am. Some miles further on, two miles offshore from Carrickfergus, the tugs were released. Captain Smith ran up the blue and white signal flag for the letter 'A' (representing 'I am undertaking sea trials') and the trials commenced. The trials were undertaken in the presence of the Board of Trade's surveyor in Belfast, Francis Carruthers, who had undertaken some 2,000 visits to Harland & Wolff's yard during the ship's construction. Carruthers was impressed by the ship's turning circle – 3,850 feet at 20.5 knots – and by the fact that she could make an emergency stop in 850 yards when travelling at 20 knots with the engines being thrown from 'Full Ahead' through 'Stop' to 'Full Astern'.

The sea trials took a single day – a fact later commented on by the US Inquiry but not the British – and, at 7.00pm, the Board of Trade Inspector requested one final action: the dropping of the port and starboard anchors. Following this, the inspector issued a certificate of seaworthiness valid for one year from 2 April 1912. With the ship having received Board of Trade certification, she was officially handed over by the shipbuilders to White Star Line.

Following her sea trials, the Titanic headed into the Irish Sea the same day at 8.00pm to make her way to Southampton and the start of her maiden voyage, with the intention that she'd reach the port during the night of 3/4 April in order to catch the midnight tide. This was destined to be the last time that she'd ever be in Belfast. During the trip to Southampton, the Titanic achieved 23.5 knots; the maximum speed that she'd

MAIN
Titanic on her sea trials in Belfast Lough.

ever attain. As she approached Southampton, she was greeted by five tugs – Ajax, Hector, Hercules, Neptune and Vulcan – owned by Red Funnel to guide her to Berth 44 in Southampton at the conclusion of her 570-mile trip from Belfast. In order to service the three great liners planned, the new deep water White Star Dock had been constructed; Olympic had already made use of these and this was to be Titanic's first and only occasion to use them. In order to maintain the weekly schedule planned for its new service, White Star Line allocated Oceanic to the service pending completion of the Gigantic.

International Mercantile Marine

Originally called the International Navigation Co, the International Mercantile Marine Co (IMM) was a trust company formed in the early 20th century. It was founded by Clement Griscom of the American and Red Star lines, Bernard Bacon of the Atlantic Transport Line, John Ellerman of Leyland Line and was bankrolled by John Pierpoint Morgan. The idea behind the company was that by co-operation, competition on the all-important transatlantic route could be reduced and thus profitability enhanced. The scale of the business was further extended by its involvement with White Star Line and J Bruce Ismay became an influential figure in the business. Although the German lines Hamburg-Amerika and North German Lloyd were not actually members of the cartel, they did co-operate with IMM in profit-sharing schemes. IMM was dissolved in 1932 with Cunard acquiring ultimately the remains of the White Star business with the US companies becoming United States Lines.

Chapter Five

The Ship's Facilities

The Titanic along with her sister ships had been designed for luxury and not directly to compete with other transatlantic liners for speed. As such, therefore, she was opulently fitted out to a standard that far exceeded any other liner then in service.

Although the Titanic had been designed as a sister ship to the Olympic, there were a number of minor variation between the

overall design of the two vessels. A number of these had been suggested by J Bruce Ismay following experience with the earlier ship. The most noticeable were that half of the Titanic's forward promenade A deck, which was located below the boat deck, was enclosed against the outside weather. Whilst the windows could be opened in the event of fine weather, normally they were kept locked. This was to have dire consequences when the ship foundered as, when the lifeboats came to be launched, the keys for opening the windows to allow those from A deck to gain access to the lifeboats were absent and valuable time was lost trying to locate them. The Titanic's B deck was also radically different, incorporating the first class Café Parisien restaurant. The feature was retro-fitted to the Olympic in 1913. There were also a number of other minor detail differences. The wheelhouse, for example, on the Titanic was longer and narrower to that fitted on the earlier ship. The result of these differences was that the Titanic weighed some 1,004 gross tons more than the Olympic.

Apart from the Café Parisien, the Titanic was also provided with a squash court, separate libraries for all three classes of passenger, a Turkish bath, gymnasium and swimming pool. The first class rooms, in particular, were lavishly fitted out; the smoking room, for example, was provided with an old rose carpet with pink drapes over the curtains. In an era when third class passengers were generally provided with poor facilities, the Titanic was unusual in that it offered reasonable facilities to this class of passenger. Apart from the third class library, there was also a smoking room, two bars and a general room for the use of third class passengers. The third class general room was located on C deck. The room was panelled

and framed in pine with a white enamel finish. The chairs in the room were made of teak and, for the men, there was a separate smoking room adjacent. This was again furnished in teak but panelled and framed in oak.

Second class rooms were located on B and C decks. The smoking room, located to the aft on B deck, was panelled in oak with oak furniture upholstered in dark green morocco leather. On C deck, the second class library was panelled in sycamore, with mahogany furniture covered in tapestries and with green silk drapes in the windows. The quality of the second class public rooms was of a standard comparable to first class on many of the competing lines.

In terms of catering on board the ship, the set meal times were one of the few areas where White Star laid down a rigid timetable. Breakfast was served to all classes between 8.30 and 10.30am. Luncheon for first and second class passengers and dinner for third class was served between 1.00pm and 2.30pm. Dinner for first and second class passengers and tea for third class was served between 6.00pm and 7.30pm. The first class dining room, with seating for 532, was situated on Deck D; the Captain's Table, with seating for six, was located amidships towards the front of the room. The first class dining room was the largest single room on board the ship. The second class dining room offered accommodation for 394 and the two third class saloons, located on Deck F, could accommodate a total of 473. First and second class ticket holders were allowed to use the à la carte restaurant on Deck B; this was run under contract by Luigi Gatti with staff drawn from his two London restaurants. If first or second class passengers elected to use the à la carte restaurant throughout the journey rather than the main dining rooms, they were offered a discount of $15-$25. The à la carte restaurant, which served hot food from 8.00am through to 11.00pm every day and which could seat 137 at 49 tables, was panelled in French walnut with a two-tone Dubarry carpet..First class passengers

MAIN
The magnificent dome covered grand staircase as depicted in this replica.

were also entitled to use the Café Parisien, which was located adjacent to the à la carte restaurant on Deck B. The Café Parisien was also staffed by employees drawn from the two restaurants owned by Gatti in London. As neither passengers nor crew, the Italian staff employed in the à la carte restaurant and Café Parisien were in an invidious position when it came to the sinking. The Café Parisien was for the exclusive use of first class passengers.

The most sumptuous part of the ship's interior was the forward first class staircase. This was located between the first and second funnels and extended down as far as E deck. Decorated with gilded balustrades and fitted with oak panelling, it was topped by an ornate dome made out of wrought iron and glass. On the uppermost landing was a large panel containing a clock supported by the allegorical figures of Glory and Honour. A second, but less ornate, staircase was located between the third and fourth panels; this was again surmounted by a glass and wrought-iron dome.

Third class sleeping accommodation – designed for 1,026 passengers – was located on the front section of Deck D and on fore and aft sections of Decks E and F. The distance between the fore and aft sections meant that the crew was able to segregate unmarried emigrants by sex. Amongst the accommodation provided for single men were 164 'open berths' (ie bunks in a dormitory).

The captain's quarters were located on the boat deck on the starboard side just aft of the wheelhouse (which stood behind the bridge). The other deck officers – Murdoch, Lightoller, etc – had their cabins in the same section; this area, known as the 'Officers' House' was built around the foremost funnel.

Apart from the actual accommodation offered to the passengers, the ship was also technologically advanced for its time. A total of three lifts were provided: two were for the use of first class passengers but, again unusually for the period, a third was provided for second class travellers. Making use of steam-powered generators, the ship was also fully fitted with electric lighting. However, the ship was not

fitted with a public address system, which would have made for more control on the night of the actual disaster. In order that the

ABOVE
Harold Bride sat in the Marconi room.

LEFT
A replica of the first class hall of Titanic.

ship could be in contact constantly with other vessels and, when in range, with land, the ship was also provided with two Marconi wireless sets. In the unfolding tragedy of April 1912, these would come into their own. The wireless room was located on the boat deck on the port side towards the aft section of the 'Officers' House'.

The normal procedure with the Marconi operation was that the Marconi operators – in the case of the Titanic Jack Phillips and Harold Bride – these were directly employed by the Marconi company – the Marconi International Marine Communications Co Ltd – and were allocated free board and lodging on board the ship in exchange for allowing the ship to send free messages between the ship and its owners, other vessels and the shore, provided that these messages never exceeded 30 words per message. The real money as far as Marconi was concerned came from the relaying of messages

to and from passengers. Again, this was to have implication on the eve of the tragedy when due to a fault in the equipment, the Marconi operators had not been able to complete the wireless transmissions.

Each of the wirelesses on board was rated at 1.5kW and each had a range of 400 miles. In order to ensure the efficient use of the system, each ship had its own distinct call sign, which also incorporated the nation of registration. For ships registered in the UK, the call sign was prefixed by the letter 'M'; for those from the USA, the prefix was 'N' and for those from Germany the letter 'D' was adopted. Thus the call signs for the Titanic and Olympic were 'MGY' and 'MKC' respectively. Whilst working the wirelesses, the radio operators would be able to hear transmissions made to and from other ships and again this would form part of the build-up to the actual collision.

Chapter Six

The Ship's Crew

Bandsmen

Apart from Wallace Hartley, whose life is detailed in more detail later, the ship's band comprised seven other musicians. These were W Theodore Brailey (aged 24), cellist Roger Marie Bricoux (aged 20), bass violinist John Frederick Preston Clarke (aged 30), violinists John Law Hume (aged 28) and Belgian,

Georges Alexandre Krins (aged 23) and cellists Percy Cornelius Taylor (aged 32) and John Wesley Woodward (aged 32).

Of the seven members other than Wallace Hartley, the bodies of two were ultimately to be recovered – Messrs Clarke and Hume – by the Mackay-Bennett and both were buried in Nova Scotia. Ironically, both Theodore Brailey and Roger Bricoux had previously been engaged on the RMS Carpathia. On board the ship, the band was normally split in two: one group of three (a pianist, cellist and violinist) played in the second class dining saloon or lounge while the remaining five played for first class passengers. The former group wore blue jackets, whilst those in first class wore white jackets and blue trousers. The division was not rigid as every member of the orchestra was expected to know every song in the company's song book and recognise instantly any of the 352 tunes by its number when announced by Hartley.

LEFT
Members of the bandsmen from Titanic.

Joseph Bell

Born in 1861 in Maryport, Cumberland, and educated in Carlisle, Bell was the Titanic's chief engineer. Having served his apprenticeship with Robert Stephenson & Co, in Newcastle upon Tyne, he started his career at sea with the Lamport & Holt Line, based in Liverpool. After two years with Lamport & Holt he joined White Star Line, serving for many years on the company's services to

New Zealand and New York. In 1891 he was promoted to be chief engineer on board the Coptic, and served on board the Olympic before being transferred to the Titanic. Married with four children, his eldest son, then aged 16 and a half, had joined Harland & Wolff as an apprentice and was with his father on board the Titanic. It was with Bell that J Bruce Ismay held discussions whilst the ship was at Queenstown about the possibility of a high-speed run on either the Monday or Tuesday. Like most of the ship's engineers, Bell was to die with the ship's sinking.

Joseph Boxhall

The Titanic's Fourth Officer was born in Hull on 23 March 1884 and started his marine career as an apprentice on 2 June 1889 with William Thomas Line of Liverpool. He joined White Star Line in 1907, serving on board the Oceanic and Arabic before being transferred to the Titanic in March 1912. At the time of the collision,

RIGHT
Joseph Boxhall.

Boxhall was off duty and near the officers' quarters but, hearing the look out bell, headed for the bridge. He was ordered by Captain Smith to undertake an inspection of the forward section of the ship and initially could find no damage. However, informed by other crew members that the ship was taking on water, he reported this back to Captain Smith.

Boxhall also calculated the position of the ship for inclusion within the distress signal and believed that he saw masthead lights from a nearby ship (often believed to be the SS California). Having roused Third Officer Pitman from his bunk, Boxhall assisted with the preparation of the lifeboats and was put in charge of lifeboat No 2 when it was lowered at 1.45am. Boxhall with the rest of the group in the lifeboat was rescued by the Carpathia. After the sinking, Boxhall continued to work for White Star Line until his retirement in1940, except for a period during World War 1 when he served with the Royal Navy. Boxhall died on 25 April 1967 and his ashes were spread over the point, 41°46N 50°14W, that he had calculated 55 years earlier to be the point at which the Titanic had sunk.

Harold Sydney Bride

One of the two radio operators on board the Titanic, Harold Bride was born in London on 11 January 1890 and joined the Marconi Company, who actually employed the wireless operators on board the White Star ships rather than the line, in 1911. He was the junior wireless operator on board the Titanic and had retired to bed during the evening of 14 April as he was due to relieve Jack Phillips at midnight, two hours earlier than normal. Following the collision with the iceberg, Bride joined Phillips in the wireless room where Phillips remained operating the wireless whilst Bride relayed messages to and from Captain Smith. As the power supply failed, Smith told Bride and Phillips that they had done their duty and that they were relieved from their posts. Bride assisted in efforts to free collapsible lifeboat B from the roof of the officers' quarters.

The lifeboat was eventually washed off and Bride found himself under the capsized lifeboat. Escaping from it, he and 15 others were to be rescued by the Carpathia from the lifeboat. Following his rescue, he assisted the Carpathia's wireless operator, Harold Cottam, in sending messages from the survivors. In New York, Bride, having been met by Guglielmo Marconi himself sold his exclusive story to the New York Times for $1000 before giving evidence to both the US and UK inquiries into the accident. Bride continued to work at sea until the early 1920s and he died on 29 April 1956.

Gaspare Antonio Pietro Gatti

Known as Luigi, Gatti was born in Montalto Pavese, in Italy, on 3 January 1875. The only member of his large family to emigrate to Britain, he married a Briton and had a family. A successful restaurateur, he ran two restaurants in London – 'Gatti's Adelphi' and 'Gatti's Strand' – and also held the concession for the à la carte first class restaurants on board both the Olympic and the Titanic, which he staffed with employees, mainly Italian, from his London establishments. A total of 68 alongside Gatti were employed by the Café Parisien; of these, the vast majority were to perish when the Titanic sunk. One of those who died was Gatti himself; his body was recovered by the Minia and he was buried in Halifax, Nova Scotia, on 10 May 1912. Any possessions that were also recovered were returned to his widow, save for a single dollar bill, from his wallet, which was sent to his family back in Italy.

LEFT
Harold Bride.

Wallace Hartley

Noted as the bandleader on board the Titanic who famously played on whilst the liner sank, Hartley was born on 2 June 1878 in the small Lancashire town of Colne. Moving to Dewsbury, in Yorkshire, he learnt to play the violin and, at the age of 31, began working for Cunard, primarily on board their liner RMS Mauretania. By 1912, he was employed by C W & F N Black, whose business it was to supply musicians to both White Star and Cunard. In April 1912, the Blacks assigned Hartley as bandmaster to the Titanic for its maiden voyage and, despite his reluctance to sail (he'd recently got engaged to Maria Robinson), he agreed to lead the eight-member band on board. Each member of the band was expected to know all 352 tunes and songs from the White Star Line's

Second Officer when the decision was made to transfer Henry Wilde from the Olympic. Born on 30 March 1874 in Chorley, Lancashire, he started his apprenticeship at the age of 13 on board the Primrose Hill. His second voyage – on board the Holt Hill – saw the ship seriously damaged in a storm and later run aground in the Indian Ocean, with the crew eventually rescued from an uninhabited island. Lightoller continued to work on sailing ships until 1895, when he transferred to Elder Dempster's Royal Mail service to Africa.

During this period he was seriously ill with malaria. After this, in 1898, he went to the Yukon as a gold prospector before becoming a cowboy in Alberta, Canada, working his passage home on a cattle boat the following year. He joined White Star Line in 1900 as Fourth Officer on board the Medic. He progressed through the ranks at

song book. Following the collision with the iceberg, Hartley and the band played music in order to help maintain some semblance of calm whilst the lifeboats were loaded. It was reported by many of the survivors that the band carried on playing as the Titanic's final moments drew on although there has always been some debate as to the final music played. Some of those who survived claimed that the band's final piece was the popular hymn 'Nearer, my God, to Thee', although Harold Bride claimed that it was another popular hymn from the period – 'Autumn' ('Songe d'Automne'). None of the band survived the sinking, although Hartley's body was recovered and he was buried in Colne.

Charles Lightoller

The most senior member of the Titanic's crew to survive, Charles Lightoller was initially appointed First Officer on board the new liner but was temporarily reduced to

White Star, becoming First Officer on board the Titanic in late March for the new liner's sea trials. On the evening of the collision with the iceberg, he had been officer of the watch immediately prior to Murdoch taking over and was retiring to bed when the ship struck. He took the view that he'd wait until summoned as, he believed, it was more sensible to remain where he was supposed to be rather than join the panic.

He was set to work assisting the allocation of passengers to lifeboats before being thrown into the sea as the ship sank. The force of one of the funnels forced him towards collapsible lifeboat B, which had been overturned. Lightoller organised the men thrown from the lifeboat thus aiding some 30 men to survive. After the sinking, Lightoller resumed his career with White Star Line briefly but, tainted by the disaster, he found it difficult to achieve promotion and he resigned shortly thereafter.

After his life at sea he had a varied career, including running a pub and property speculation. Lightoller was to serve with distinction during both World War 1 – where he was awarded the Distinguished Service Cross and bar – and World War 2, where he commanded one of the 'Little Ships' that helped rescue British and Allied soldiers from the beaches of Dunkirk in 1940. He died on 8 December 1952.

MAIN
Look-out point, seen here on the front mast of the Titanic.

Look-outs

There were six look-outs on board the Titanic, of which four were directly involved in the unfolding tragedy: Alfred Evans, Frederick Fleet, George Hogg, Archie Jewell, Reginald Lee and George Symons. Alfred Frank Evans was born in Hampshire and was 24 when he transferred from the Oceanic to the Titanic. Having been on duty from 6.00pm to 8.00pm, Evans and Hogg were due to relieve Fleet and Lee at midnight. Although the ship had by this time hit the iceberg, the change was properly effected although Evans and Hogg remained up the crow's nest for only 20 minutes before heading for the boat deck.

Evans was one of the crew members who escaped on board lifeboat No 15. He died in 1974. Frederick Fleet, born in Liverpool on 15 October 1887, was brought up as an orphan, before joining a training ship at the age of 12. Following training, he went to sea in 1903, starting work as a deck boy, before being promoted to Able Seaman. He had worked as a look-out on board the Oceanic for four years before transferring to the Titanic. It was Fleet, in the crow's nest with Reginald Lee, who spotted the iceberg and endeavoured to warn the bridge.

Having been relieved, Fleet assisted Quartermaster Hitchens crew lifeboat No 6 and was thus to be picked up by the Carpathia. Following his survival, Fleet continued with White Star until August 1912 – the company tended to regard the surviving officers and crew as unfortunate reminders of the tragedy – and then transferred to Union-Castle. He continued at sea until 1936 and then worked for a period at Harland & Wolff. Fleet committed suicide on 10 January 1965 shortly after the death of his wife and having been evicted by his brother-

in-law. George Alfred Hogg was born on 7 March 1883 in Hull and first went to sea in 1899. He transferred to the Titanic from the Dongola. He had done the 6.00pm to 8.00pm shift with Alfred Evans and was, therefore, in bed when the iceberg struck. Due on duty again at midnight, he dressed and, with Evans, headed for the crow's nest. They remained on duty for 20 minutes before descending to the boat deck to assist in the loading of the lifeboats. Hogg was ordered by Murdoch to assist the crewing of lifeboat No 7.

It was Hogg at the British inquiry that raised the question of the lack of binoculars in the crow's nest.

Archie Jewell was born on 4 December 1888 in Bude, Cornwall and first went to sea when he was aged 15. He joined White Star Line in 1904 and had served on board the Oceanic for some seven years before he was transferred to the Titanic in April 1912. He had been on duty until 10.00pm when he was relieved by Fleet and Lee and was in his berth when the collision took place as his next duty was due to commence at 4.00am. He was one of the crew members on board lifeboat No 7, which was lowered at 12.45am, and was picked up by the Carpathia at 4.10am. After the sinking, Jewell testified to the British inquiry, being thanked by Lord Mersey for answering some 331 questions. Jewell returned to the sea after the tragedy and was to be killed on 17 April 1917 when the SS Donegal was torpedoed by a German submarine some 19 miles south of the Dean Light Vessel in the English Channel. Reginald Robinson Lee was born on 19 May 1870 in Oxfordshire. His family moved to Hampshire whilst he was a child. Prior to serving on board the Titanic Lee had previously served as look-

LEFT
George Hogg.

out on the Olympic. With Fleet when the iceberg was spotted, Lee was eventually to escape the sinking ship on board lifeboat No 13. After testifying to the Board of Trade inquiry, he returned to sea; however, he was not to outlive the sinking long as he died of pneumonia on 6 August 1913 whilst serving on board the Kenilworth Castle.

George Thomas Macdonald Symons was born in Weymouth, Dorset on 23 February 1888 and, like a number of others, had served on board the Oceanic before transferring to the Titanic. He had been on duty until 10.00pm and was also in his berth when the ship struck. He was to be put in charge of lifeboat No 1 – the infamous 'Millionaires' Boat' on which the Duff-Gordon party made their escape.

Harold Godfrey Lowe

Born near Conwy, in North Wales, on 21 November 1882, Harold Godfrey was the Fifth Officer on board the Titanic. At the age of 14 he ran away to sea, initially working on Welsh coasters whilst he learnt the trade, achieving his Second Mate's Certificate in 1906 and his First Mate's Certificate two years later. He joined White Star Line in 1911 working on the Belgic and Tropic before being transferred to the Titanic in March 1912.

On the night of the collision, Lowe had been on duty until 8pm and was soundly asleep when the iceberg was struck, not waking until something approaching 30 minutes after the accident had happened. Appraised of the position he got dressed, grabbed his revolver and started to assist in the lowering of the lifeboats. Whilst working to lower lifeboat No 5, Lowe had an altercation with J Bruce Ismay, who was urging greater speed. At about 1.30am,

Lowe and Moody agreed that each should take charge of one of the surviving lifeboats, with Lowe taking control of No 14. The launching of the lifeboat was precarious, given the angle of the ship, and Lowe was forced to fire his revolver three times to prevent passengers endangering the lifeboat in their panic.

With lifeboat No 14 safely launched, Lowe gathered together a number of lifeboats and, as the ship sank, determined to try to return to the scene to rescue those still in the water but was overruled by those already on board who feared that additional survivors would swamp the lifeboats. Eventually, after the majority had died down, Lowe returned to the scene and plucked a handful of additional survivors from the water. Lowe next turned his attention to collapsible lifeboat A, which was in danger of sinking,

and saved those on board. Lowe, with the rest of those with him, was rescued by the Carpathia on the morning of 15 April. Lowe served with the Royal Naval Reserve during World War 1 and died on 12 May 1944.

James Paul Moody

Born on 21 August 1887 in Scarborough, Yorkshire, James Moody was the Sixth Officer on board the Titanic. He started his life at sea at the nautical training ship, HMS Conway, in Birkenhead in 1901 before joining White Star Line. He served on the Oceanic before being transferred to the Titanic in March 1912. He was on duty between 8pm and midnight and so was on the bridge with First Officer Murdoch when the look-out, Frederick Fleet, reported the sighting of the iceberg and sounded the warning bell three times.

It was Moody who took Fleet's call asking the look-out what he had seen and receiving the response 'Iceberg, right ahead'. Following the collision, Moody was employed in assisting with the launching of lifeboats 12, 14 and 16 and, as the ship's condition deteriorated, discussed with Fifth Officer Lowe the need for an officer to be on board each of the lifeboats as it was launched. Lowe took lifeboat No 14, which was successfully launched, but Moody, allocated No 16, was not so lucky. He was last spotted trying, with others, to launch collapsible lifeboat A and died as the ship sank.

William McMaster Murdoch

Initially appointed Chief Officer of the Titanic, Murdoch was reduced to the post of First Officer when it was decided that Henry Wilde would take over as Chief Officer shortly before the ship set sail. Born in southwest Scotland on 28 February 1873,

Murdoch was in command of the Titanic during those fateful moments when the iceberg was spotted and then struck. Coming from a seafaring family, Murdoch moved to Liverpool at the age of 14 to become an apprentice with William Joyce & Co. His ability was such that he passed his Second Mate's Certificate after only four years. Initially he served on board the Charles Cosworth, a vessel involved in trade with South America. In 1896 he gained his Extra Master's Certificate and in 1900 joined White Star Line.

As Second Officer on board the Arabic in 1903, Murdoch had been instrumental in ensuring the ship avoided a collision in the dark. In May 1911 Murdoch was appointed First Officer of the Olympic and was Docking Officer at the stern of the ship when it was rammed by HMS Hawke on 20 September 1911. Following repairs, Murdoch rejoined the ship on 11 December 1911. In April 1912 he was appointed Chief Officer on the Titanic, but was made First Officer with Wilde's transfer. As officer in charge during the night of 14 April, he gave the commands 'full speed astern' and 'hard a starboard' when the iceberg was sighted. Once the ship started to sink, Murdoch was put in charge of evacuation on the starboard side; he was last seen trying to release collapsible lifeboat A. He died during the sinking and his body was never recovered.

Herbert John Pitman

Born on 20 November 1877 near Castle Cary in Somerset, Bert Pitman was the Third Officer on board the Titanic. He was the only senior officer on board who was not also a member of the Royal Naval Reserve. He joined the merchant navy in 1895 and qualified as a master mariner in August 1906,

the same year in which he joined White Star Line. He joined the Titanic in Belfast in late March 1912.

At the time of the accident, he was off duty and in his bunk in the officers' quarters; following the collision he was ordered to assist in the preparation of the lifeboats on the starboard side. Murdoch ordered Pitman to take charge of lifeboat No 5. The lifeboat was not full and Pitman had been ordered to take more passengers on via the gangway doors; however, these were closed and no more passengers were taken on board. Pitman moved the lifeboat some 400 yards away from the ship as the Titanic sank but, hearing the cries of those in the water, ordered the lifeboat crew back towards the site.

The crew, however, fearing that the lifeboat would get overloaded refused and Pitman reluctantly rescinded his order. It was a decision that he'd regret for the rest of his life. Pitman and the other survivors on board lifeboat No 5 were rescued by the Carpathia. After the sinking, Pitman carried on with his career, working with White Star Line until the early 1920s when he joined Shaw, Savill & Albion Co Ltd. He finally retired in 1946 and died on 7 December 1961.

John George Phillips

'Jack' Phillips was the senior of the two Marconi-employed wireless operators on board the Titanic. Born in Surrey on 11 April 1887, Phillips first joined the Marconi Company in March 1906. Prior to joining the Titanic in April 1912, he had served on a range of ships, including the Cunard-owned Lusitania and Mauretania. During the day of 14 April 1912 the wireless had failed and, during the evening, Phillips was on duty trying to catch up with messages that had accumulated from earlier in the day. Whilst on duty, Phillips received a number of warnings about the presence of ice in the area, the most pertinent being from the Californian at 11.00pm. Following the collision with the iceberg, Phillips was joined by his junior Harold Bride as they sought to continue issuing calls for assistance and 'SOS' messages until the power gradually faded and the water rose. Following Captain Smith's instruction that they were relieved of their duties, both Phillips and Bride sought to make good their escape; unfortunately, another crew member had attempted to steal Phillips' life jacket. Bride spotted this and held the miscreant whilst Phillips knocked the man out. There is some dispute as to Phillips' fate; according to some he was on board collapsible lifeboat B but died before the Carpathia picked up the survivors. Others believe, however, that he failed to make it to

the lifeboat. In any event, Phillips died during the sinking and, as a result of his efforts in trying to maintain contact for as long as possible, is widely regarded as one of the heroes of the night.

Edward John Smith

The captain of the Titanic, Captain Edward Smith, nicknamed 'E J' by fellow officers in the Merchant Navy, was one of White Star Line's most experienced officers, although his career had not been without incident. Smith was born on 27 January 1850 at Hanley, Stoke-on-Trent – not a place traditionally associated with seafaring men.

His father was a potter and his parents later owned a shop. At the age of 13 Smith headed to Liverpool and became apprenticed to Gibson & Co. He joined White Star Line in March 1880, initially as Fourth Officer on board the Celtic. In 1887, he achieved his first command, when he became captain on board the SS Republic. In 1888, Smith earned his Extra Master's Certificate and, with it, a commission as a Lieutenant in the Royal Naval Reserve. His rank in the RNR permitted him to fly the blue ensign of the RNR rather than the red ensign of the merchant marine.

In 1895, Smith was appointed as captain of the Majestic, serving for nine years in this role during which time the ship was pressed into use as a troop ship carrying British soldiers to South Africa for the Boer War for which service Smith was awarded the Transport Medal by King Edward II.

Following his appointment as Commodore of the White Star Line in 1904, it became usual practice for Smith to take command of the line's newest vessels. He was thus appointed captain of the Baltic in 1904, taking her on the ship's maiden voyage to New York on 29 June 1904. In 1907, he transferred to the next major new liner, the Adriatic, and, in 1911, took command of the RMS Olympic.

The Olympic's maiden voyage passed without incident until she reached New York on 21 June 1911 when, in trying to dock at Pier 59 with the assistance of the harbour pilot and 12 tugs, one of the tugs collided with the Olympic and was trapped temporarily under the larger vessel's stern. This was not the only accident to affect the Olympic whilst under Smith's command: on 20 September 1911 she was rammed

by HMS Hawke, which resulted in the liner returning to Belfast for repair, and, in February 1912, she lost a propeller blade, again being forced to return to Belfast for repair. Smith's next command was the Titanic itself and he boarded the vessel in Southampton on 10 April 1912 ready for the ship's maiden voyage. Smith's fate, other than he died when the ship sank, is unknown; his body was never recovered.

Henry Tingle Wilde

The Chief Officer on board the Titanic, Wilde was born on 21 September 1872 in Walton, Liverpool, and was apprenticed to James Chambers & Co of Liverpool on 23 October 1889. Initially he served on board the Greystoke Castle, becoming the ship's Third Mate.

He then served on board the Hornby Castle, the SS Brunswick – his first experience on board a steamship – and the SS Europa before joining White Star Line in July 1897. Remaining with White Star Line for the remainder of his career, he gradually progressed through the ranks until his appointment as Chief Officer aboard the Olympic in August 1911, where he served under Captain Smith.

He followed Smith to the Titanic for the new liner's maiden voyage but was not initially destined to serve on board the new ship. He had been originally ordered to sail with the Olympic on 3 April but was transferred, probably at Smith's request, to the Titanic, where he replaced Murdoch as Chief Officer (Murdoch thus became First Officer and Charles Lightoller Second Officer; the original Second Officer, David Blair, didn't sail with the Titanic – a fortunate escape in the light of history). At the time that the iceberg was struck, Wilde was off duty but was roused and assisted with the loading of the even numbered lifeboats on the port side.

He was seen trying to detach the collapsible lifeboats A and B from the roof of the officers' quarters. Wilde was not to survive.

RIGHT
Henry Wilde.

Chapter Seven

Notable Passengers

John Jacob Astor IV

Coming from one of the wealthiest families in the USA, Astor was born on 13 July 1864 and was to be the wealthiest man to die on board the Titanic. The family had interests in the fur trade,

real estate, hotels and much else, but Astor himself was more than a simple businessman. He had served in the army as a Lieutenant-Colonel during the Spanish-American War and had also written a science-fiction novel – *A Journey to Other Worlds* – in 1894. He was also an inventor with several patented inventions. On 11 September 1911 the 47-year-old Astor married Madeleine Talmadge Force, who was then 18 years old (and younger than Astor's own son Vincent). In order to allow the scandal to decline in the USA, Astor and his new wife travelled to Europe. During the course of their travels she became pregnant and Astor desired to have the baby born in the USA. As a result, they booked themselves on the Titanic's maiden voyage and boarded the vessel at Cherbourg.

The Astor party – which included two servants and a nurse – occupied the 'parlour suite' (C62 – which was decorated in a Louis XIV style) with the nurse, Caroline Endres, in C45. This consisted of a sitting room, two bedrooms, bathroom with toilet, and two storage rooms. Once the ship struck the iceberg, Astor ensured that his wife, and a fellow traveller Molly Brown, were allocated a place on board a lifeboat and, mentioning that his wife was pregnant, sought to board

LEFT
Madeleine Astor, wife of John.

the boat as well. When told that it was women and children first, he stood back. Astor seems to have been crushed when No 1 Funnel collapsed; his body, covered in soot, was recovered on 22 April and was buried in New York. His wife and Molly Brown both survived. Astor's body was recovered and was one of the first to be claimed when the Mackay-Bennett docked at Halifax, Nova Scotia, having searched the area for bodies.

Thomas Andrews

Born on 7 February 1873, Andrews was the managing director and head of the draughting department at Harland & Wolff when the 'Olympic' class ships were ordered. At the age of 16, following five years of study at the Royal Belfast Academical Institution, he joined the shipyard as a premium apprentice. His uncle, William James Pirrie, was part owner of the yard and, following Harland's death in 1894, was to become the company's chairman.

At Harland & Wolff, Andrews made steady progress through the company, being appointed manager of the construction works in 1901 before being appointed managing director and head of the draughting department six years later. The same year, 1907, saw the yard commissioned to construct the first of White Star Line's new 'Olympic' class liners. The ships were designed by Andrews in conjunction with Pirrie and Alexander Carlisle. As was usual, Andrews led a party of Harland & Wolff personnel on board each vessel's maiden voyage and the sailing of the Titanic in April 1912 was no different.

He was allocated first class cabin A 36 on the port side. Roused after the ship hit the lifeboat to assess the damage alongside

Captain Smith, Andrews, having seen the mail bags from the post room floating 24 feet above the keel, realised both that the vessel was doomed and that there was inadequate provision of lifeboats for all passengers and crew. During the ship's last hours he spent the time rousing passengers in order to get them to put life jackets on and head for the lifeboat stations. Andrews was last spotted standing in the first-class smoking room in front of a painting showing the entrance to Plymouth Sound; he is presumed to have perished as the ship sank.

Lawrence Beesley

Not one of the rich and famous on board the Titanic, Beesley was a schoolmaster whose prominence arose as a result of his book – *The Loss of the SS Titanic: Its Story and its Lessons by One of the Survivors* – which was published in June 1912. Beesley was born in

to die, aged 89, on 14 April 1967 – exactly
55 years after the ship sank.

Karl Howell Behr

Born on 30 May 1885, Behr was a US lawyer
but was perhaps better known as a tennis
player, playing for the USA in the Davis Cup
and in the Men's Doubles at Wimbledon.
He was aboard the Titanic in pursuit of his
courtship of Helen Monypeny Newsom;
Miss Newsom's mother disapproved of the
romance and had taken her daughter to
Europe to escape Behr's attentions.

Manufacturing an excuse for a business
trip to Europe, Behr booked himself on
the Titanic – first class cabin C148 –
from Cherbourg in order to continue his
relationship. On the night of the sinking,
Behr was in the company of Miss Newsom
and others and went with them to the
starboard boat deck. Although Third Officer

Wirksworth, Derbyshire, on 31 December
1877 and educated at Derby School and
then at Caius College, Cambridge, where
he obtained a First Class Degree in Natural
Science in 1903. Following a period teaching
in Wirksworth, he was, by the time of the
sinking, employed at Dulwich College in
London. He was a second class passenger,
allocated cabin No D56, and commented on
the collision with the iceberg that it was 'a
more than usual dancing of the mattress on
which I sat. Nothing more than that – no
sound of a crash or of anything else; no sense
of shock, no jar that felt like one heavy body
meeting another.' Beesley was to escape on
lifeboat No 13 when he was asked if there
were any women and children around as
the boat was being launched by the crew
member in charge. Replying in the negative,
Beesley was told to get on board. Beesley was

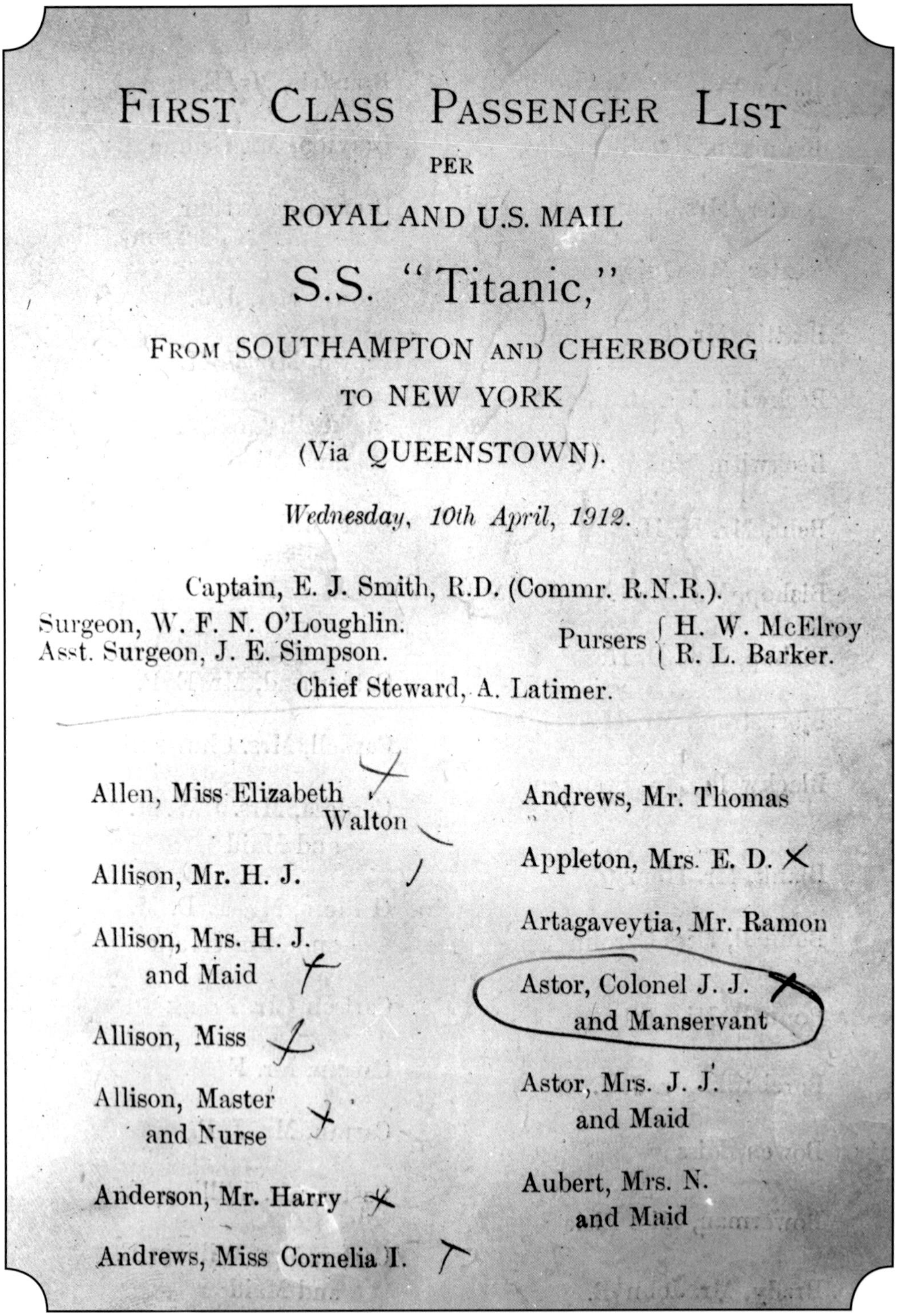

LEFT
Sample of the first
class passenger list.

FIRST CLASS PASSENGER LIST

PER

ROYAL AND U.S. MAIL

S.S. "Titanic,"

FROM SOUTHAMPTON AND CHERBOURG

TO NEW YORK

(Via QUEENSTOWN).

Wednesday, 10th April, 1912.

Captain, E. J. Smith, R.D. (Commr. R.N.R.).

Surgeon, W. F. N. O'Loughlin.
Asst. Surgeon, J. E. Simpson.

Pursers { H. W. McElroy.
{ R. L. Barker.

Chief Steward, A. Latimer.

Allen, Miss Elizabeth
          Walton

Allison, Mr. H. J.

Allison, Mrs. H. J.
    and Maid

Allison, Miss

Allison, Master
    and Nurse

Anderson, Mr. Harry

Andrews, Miss Cornelia I.

Andrews, Mr. Thomas

Appleton, Mrs. E. D.

Artagaveytia, Mr. Ramon

Astor, Colonel J. J.
    and Manservant

Astor, Mrs. J. J.
    and Maid

Aubert, Mrs. N.
    and Maid

Pitman was trying to ensure 'women and children first', one of the party – Mrs Kimball enquired whether all could board lifeboat No 5; J Bruce Ismay, who was assisting Pitman, concurred and so the entire party, including Behr, boarded. Behr was one of a committee of survivors – the others included Frederick K Seward (the chairman), Molly Brown, Frederic Oakley Spedden and George Harder – to honour the bravery of Captain Rostron and the crew of the Carpathia. They presented an engraved silver cup to the captain and medals to each of the 320 crew members. Both Behr and Miss Newsom survived and were married the following year. Behr later went into banking before his death on 15 October 1949.

Francis M Browne SJ

Later to be ordained a Catholic priest, Browne was born on 3 July 1880 in Cork and underwent schooling in Ireland, leaving in 1897. He then went on a tour of Europe before becoming a Jesuit novitiate. After this he became a student at the Royal University Dublin, being an exact contemporary of James Joyce, the novelist. After finishing his studies at Dublin, he spent the years between 1902 and 1906 studying philosophy in Italy. He entered theological training in 1911 and, the following year, his uncle paid for him to make the trip from Southampton to Queenstown on board the Titanic.

He sailed from Queenstown to Holyhead on 8 April, travelling by train from there to London and thence to Southampton. Allocated first class room A38, Browne's importance to the story of the Titanic was that he was a pioneering and obsessive photographer – by his death in 1960 he had taken some 42,000 photographs – and

during his time on board the Titanic he compiled a unique record of the ship. Amongst the images that he took were views of the near miss with the New York as the Titanic departed from Southampton as well as portraits of a number of the prominent people on board, including the last known photograph of Captain Smith. Browne was ordained a priest on 31 July 1915 and, during World War 1, served as a chaplain with the Irish Guards; injured five times – including once being severely affected by gas – he was awarded the Military Cross and bar as well as the Croix de Guerre.

Archibald Willingham Butt

Major Archie Butt, born on 26 September 1865, was a prominent military aide to both President William Howard Taft and to President Theodore Roosevelt, having served as an officer during the Spanish-American War of 1898. He served in the Philippines between 1900 and 1906 in Cuba, before becoming Roosevelt's aide in 1908.

Following a deterioration in his health as a result of trying to mediate between Roosevelt and Taft, Butt had undertaken a six-week break in Europe with his friend Francis Millet. Having boarded at Southampton, Butt was allocated first class cabin No B38. He was one of the guests at the Wideners' private party on the evening of 14 April and after this played cards and drank with fellow passengers, including Frank Millet, Hugh Woolner and Clarence Moore, in the first class smoking room on Deck A. (Normally, White Star Line rules precluded the playing of cards on the Sabbath, but this rule had been relaxed on this occasion by the steward.) Butt was not to survive the sinking nor was his body recovered.

Sir Cosmo Edmund Duff-Gordon

The fifth Baronet of Halkin was born on 22 July 1862 and married Mrs James Stuart Wallace, a divorcee, in 1900. The family's title had come from military service during the Napoleonic Wars and had owned a sherry bodega in Spain since 1772; the family name was also carried by a well-known brand of gin. Duff-Gordon was a prominent sportsman – he represented Great Britain for fencing, for example – and landowner.

Sir Cosmo and Lady Duff-Gordon were to become infamous survivors of the Titanic by escaping in a lifeboat designed for 40 with only three friends and seven crew members although the subsequent enquiries exonerated them from any criticism. Curiously, having boarded at Cherbourg, the Duff-Gordons were booked under the name of 'Morgan' and occupied separate rooms, with Sir Cosmo in A16 and his wife in A20. Duff-Gordon with his wife and friends were waiting by lifeboat No 1 when Duff-Gordon asked First Officer Lowe if he and his party could board the lifeboat. Given confirmation that he could, the group boarded the lifeboat along with the Duff-Gordon's secretary, Miss Laura Mabel Francatelli (who was in cabin E36).

Chief Officer Murdoch, conscious that three male passengers would be unable to control the lifeboat ordered seven crew members on board as well and the boat was lowered. Although Duff-Gordon was aware of the tradition of women and children first, he contended – and he was supported in this by other survivors – that none were present when the boat was launched. The five passengers and seven crew members were safely rescued by the Carpathia. Duff-Gordon's reputation was besmirched, however, by the fact that he had offered each of the seven crew members £5 to replace their lost kit; this had been prompted by the complaints of one of the seven crew – fireman Robert W Pusey – that they had lost everything in the sinking but appeared to others more like a bribe, particularly as Duff-Gordon's agent offered further inducements to the seven prior to the two enquiries. Duff-Gordon died on 20 April 1931.

BELOW
Sir Cosmo Edmund Duff-Gordon (far right) with members of the British Fencing team.

RIGHT
Archibald Gracie.

Archibald Gracie

Allocated stateroom C51, Colonel Archibald Gracie was a military historian who was returning home to Washington DC having undertaken research in Britain on the 1812 war between Britain and the USA. Amongst his books was a history of the US Civil War. Born on 17 January 1859, Gracie attended West Point Military academy before being

commissioned into the 7th Cavalry. He boarded the Titanic at Southampton and spent much of the voyage in the company of single women, a number of whom were friends of his or his wife and who had been attending a funeral. On the evening of the sinking, he had retired to bed when he was awoken by a jolt; dressing, he ascended to the boat deck where he assisted the women that he had been chaperoning into lifeboats.

Following the launch of the last lifeboat at around 1.55am, Gracie and his friend Clinch Smith – who didn't survive – helped Lightoller and others free the four collapsible lifeboats. C and D were released before the water swept over the bridge, with B being released by the force of the water. As the ship started to sink, Gracie was drawn down by the undertow but managed to free himself and swim to the surface. Along with a couple of dozen or so, he was able to get on board lifeboat B. As dawn approached, Lightoller used his whistle to attract the other lifeboats and the weary occupants of B were transferred to boats 4 and 12; Gracie made it to No 12 from where he was later transferred to the Carpathia.

After returning to New York, Gracie undertook research into the sinking with a view to publication – his *The Truth about the Titanic* was published in 1913 – but his health had suffered as a result of prolonged exposure to the cold water and hypothermia and he died on 4 December 1912.

Dorothy Gibson

Born Dorothy Winifred Brown on 17 May 1889 in Hoboken, New Jersey, Dorothy Gibson was a noted actress in the American silent film industry. Apart from her film work, she also appeared on the stage, most notably in Charles Frohman's musical of 1907, *The Dairymaids*.

Following her marriage to George Battier Jr in 1909, she also became well-known as the model used by the commercial artist Harrison Fisher. Her first appearance in films occurred in *Miss Masquerader* (1911), *Hands Across the Sea* (1911) and *Love Finds a Way* (1912), being equally adept in either comedy or drama roles. She was on board the Titanic returning from Italy where she had been on holiday with her mother.

On the night of the collision, the two women had been playing bridge with others in the lounge; when the boat struck the iceberg, they made their way to the boat deck and managed to escape on board lifeboat No 7, the first to be launched. Arriving back with the other survivors on board the Carpathia, she was encouraged by her manager, Pat Casey, to write and to

star in a film about the sinking. *Saved from the Titanic* was released in 1912 and, in the film, she wore the same clothing – a white silk evening dress with cardigan and polo coat – that she'd worn during her actual escape. Dorothy Gibson retired from film making shortly after the making of *Saved from the Titanic*, and following her divorce from Battier (from whom she had already been separated) in 1916, she married Jules Brulatour, one of the founders of Universal Studios in 1917, although the marriage was annulled two years later. Following this, she emigrated to France where she spent the rest of her life apart from a four-year period in Italy during World War 2 (where she was for a time imprisoned before escaping). She died on 17 February 1946.

Benjamin Guggenheim

The fifth son of the mining magnate Meyer Guggenheim, Benjamin Guggenheim was born on 26 October 1865. Based for much of the time in France, Guggenheim, who was estranged from his wife, boarded the Titanic at Cherbourg on 10 April along with his mistress, the French singer Léontine Aubart, her maid, Emma Sägesser, his valet, Victor Giglio and his chauffeur, René Pernot.

Guggenheim and Giglio occupied cabin B82 whilst the two women occupied B35; the chauffeur was allocated a berth in second class. When awakened, both Guggenheim and Giglio were initially reluctant to believe that the ship had struck an iceberg but took action to get the women on board lifeboat No 9, although Guggenheim reassured the maid in German that 'It's just a repair. Tomorrow the Titanic will go on again', he was aware of the serious position in which the ship found itself. With the women safely

ensconced on the lifeboat, Guggenheim and Giglio adjourned back to their cabin to change into evening wear. He was heard to comment 'We've dressed up in our best and are prepared to go down like gentlemen'. Guggenheim, Giglio and Pernot all perished as the ship sank, with their bodies never being recovered; both women survived, ironically dying within months of each other 52 years later.

Henry Birkhardt Harris

Harris, born in St Louis, Missouri, on 1 December 1866 was a theatrical impresario and manager, who managed for a period Lily Langtry and Amelia Bingham and turned Robert Edeson into a star. Amongst theatres that he managed were the Hudson and the Harris and, during the 1910-11 season, had no fewer than 18 companies on tour. He and his wife boarded the Titanic in Southampton and were allocated first class cabin C83. Harris was to die when the ship sank and his body was never recovered. His wife, Irene, who was born on 15 June 1876, was to survive, however, as one of those on board collapsible D. On her return to New York, Mrs Harris discovered that her husband was effectively broke; however, she endeavoured to pay off his debts and keep the theatrical business going. She was successful in this until the Great Depression when the business finally failed. She died on 2 September 1969.

Joseph Bruce Ismay

Born on 12 December 1862, by the time of the Titanic's maiden voyage, Ismay had risen to become the managing director of White Star Line, the shipping company founded by his father Thomas Ismay. Having lost out with John Pierpoint Morgan for control of White Star Line, Ismay became chairman and managing director of International Mercantile Marine in early 1904.

It was Bruce Ismay's desire to compete more effectively with Cunard on the transatlantic run that led him in 1907 to commission Harland & Wolff to construct the three 'Olympic' class ships. Ismay decided to sail on Titanic's maiden voyage – he was allocated suite B52 that was previously booked by Henry C Frick and then John Pierpoint Morgan (both of whom had cancelled before the ship's departure – and, following the ship's collision, was to survive as one of the passengers on board collapsible lifeboat C before being transferred to the Carpathia and finally reaching New York on 18 April 1912. Following his survival when women and children had perished, Ismay was roundly criticised in both Britain and the United States, earning the nickname 'J Brute Ismay' although the evidence would suggest that he was active in encouraging as many as possible on board the lifeboats before being himself encouraged to board when he was assured there were no female passengers in the vicinity. As managing director of White Star Line he testified to both the British and US enquiries. He resigned as president of the International Mercantile Marine in 1913 although was to remain active in shipping circles thereafter. He was to die on 15 October 1937.

Francis Davis Millet

A painter and writer, born on 3 November 1846 in Massachusetts, Millet had accompanied his friend Archie Butt during the latter's six-week sojourn to Europe, but joined the ship at Cherbourg rather than Southampton. An inveterate traveller, Millet had been a war correspondent during the Russian-Turkish War and had been decorated by both Romania and Russia for his bravery. Allocated first class cabin E38, Millet wrote a letter to a friend, posted from Queenstown, in which he wrote 'Queer lot of people on the ship. There are a number of obnoxious, ostentatious American women, the scourge of any place they infest and worse on shipboard than anywhere.' He added on the number of passengers that had brought pets with them: 'Many of them carry tiny dogs, and lead husbands around like pet lambs.' Millet was one of the party that played cards and drank in the first class smoking room. As with his friend Archie Butt, Millet was not to survive the sinking, although his body was ultimately recovered by the Mackay-Bennett and his body was buried in Massachusetts. Examples of Millet's work can be found in London's Tate Gallery and in New York's Metropolitan Museum, amongst others.

Thomas William Stead

A noted journalist, who had found notoriety when he had 'bought' Eliza Armstrong, the 13-year-old daughter of a chimneysweep in 1885 as part of his campaign to end child prostitution in Britain. Stead had been born on 5 July 1849 becoming editor of the Northern Echo in Darlington when he was 22 before moving in 1880 to become assistant editor of the *Pall Mall Gazette*.

When the then editor, John Morley, moved on to become a Member of Parliament in 1883, Stead became editor. He held the post until 1889. Although Stead's campaign resulted in the passing of the Criminal Law Amendment Act in 1885, which raised the age of consent to 16, Stead was prosecuted and convicted, serving three

months in prison. After he ceased to be editor of the *Pall Mall Gazette* he continued in journalism and became increasingly prominent as a peace campaigner. He was on board the Titanic as he had been invited by President William Howard Taft to address a peace congress due to be held at the Carnegie Hall in New York on 21 April.

Earlier in his career, Stead had warned, in an article in the *Pall Mall Gazette* of 22 March 1886, of the dangers of major loss of life following a mid-Atlantic collision if the vessels concerned lacked sufficient lifeboats, and six years later, he wrote a fictional account of the sinking of a transatlantic liner sinking after a collision with an iceberg in the 1892 Christmas edition of *Review of Reviews*. He was also heavily influenced by his belief in the spirit world; despite this, however, he was to sail on the Titanic. Following the collision, Stead assisted a number of women and children into lifeboats; after this, he was last spotted sitting in the First Class Smoking Room reading a book. He was to die as the ship sank.

Isidor Straus

A German by birth and born on 6 February 1845, by the time that he was booked to travel across the Atlantic on the maiden voyage Isidor Straus – also known as Isadore Strauss – had become a prominent businessman based in the USA following his family's emigration to the States when he was nine years old. He was co-owner of Macy's, the famous department store, and also served briefly between 1894 and 1895 as a member of Congress. In 1871, he married Rosalie Ida Blun, to whom he was devoted; their mutual devotion was to cost them their lives when the Titanic sank in 1912. Mr and Mrs Straus were allocated cabin C55; this was decorated in the Regency style. As the liner was stricken, Ida Straus was offered a berth on a lifeboat; she refused telling her husband 'We have been together for many years. Where you go, I go'. The officer commanding the lifeboat, Lightoller, offered

RIGHT
Thomas William Stead.

a place to Isidor Straus, following pressure from Colonel Gracie on grounds of Straus's age, as well, but Straus declined as he did not wish to have preferential treatment. The couple's maid, Ellen Bird, was persuaded to board the lifeboat but Ida continued to refuse commenting that the couple had lived together and would die together. Straus's body was recovered and buried in New York; that of his wife was never found.

John Borland Thayer

Born on 21 April 1862, John B Thayer, with his wife Marian and son John (known as Jack), boarded the Titanic at Cherbourg after spending time with the American consul general in Berlin. Thayer was a vice-president of the Pennsylvania Railroad and, apart from Jack, he and his wife had three other children. Allocated first class cabins C-68 and C-70, the Thayers were guests at the party held by the Wideners on the evening of Sunday 14 April. Following the party, they had retired to their cabin and were preparing for bed when the collision occurred.

Jack, dressed in an overcoat over his pyjamas, went on deck to investigate and, when he reported back, all three went on deck, Jack having changed into a tweed suit with several vests in order to keep warm. Marian Thayer was to escape the sinking on lifeboat No 4 but John B Thayer, in the company of George and Harry Widener and Charles Duane Williams, remained on board to await their fate; his body was never discovered. Jack Thayer, then aged 17, was not allocated a lifeboat berth and got separated from his parents, and as the ship sank, being a strong swimmer, he decided to leap overboard and try to swim for safety. Once in the water, he eventually reached

the upturned collapsible B and joined a number of other survivors on board. As with the others on board 'B' he was rescued by lifeboats Nos 4 and 12; ironically, whilst his mother was on lifeboat No 4, Jack was allocated No 12 as neither was in a condition to recognise the other.

Jack was to board the Carpathia once lifeboat No 12 came alongside at about 8.30am and he and his mother returned home to Haverford, Pennsylvania. The sinking of the Titanic was not the only tragedy to affect Jack Thayer; one of his two sons was killed during World War 2 and this, combined with depression, caused him to commit suicide on 20 September 1945.

George Dunton Widener

One of a number of prominent American businessmen to die on board the Titanic, Widener was born on 10 June 1861 in Philadelphia, the son of the wealthy entrepreneur Peter A B Widener. Having joined his father's business, Widener took control of the Philadelphia Traction Co, and was prominent in the development of streetcar operation elsewhere in the USA.

Married to Eleanor Elkins in 1883, Widener, his wife and eldest son Harry E Widener (born in 1885), were booked on board the Titanic from Cherbourg following a holiday in Paris. On the night of the sinking, it was a party being hosted by the Widener family that Captain Smith attended. Following the collision, Widener arranged for his wife and her maid to be placed in one of the lifeboats; both the women were eventually rescued by the Carpathia and made it back to New York. Neither Widener nor his son, however, survived and their bodies were never recovered.

Chapter Eight

Other Major Figures

Alexander Montgomery Carlisle

The designer of the 'Olympic' class in conjunction with Thomas Andrews and Lord Pirrie, the Right Honourable Alexander 'Alick' Carlisle – he had been created a member of the Privy Council by Edward VII – had retired from Harland & Wolff in June 1910. Born in 1854 he joined Harland & Wolff in 1870 ultimately becoming the yard's general manager, he was one of the foremost ship designers of the period. One of his earlier

vessels was the White Star Line Teutonic, which was launched in 1889 and which became – with her sister ship – the Majestic – the last White Star Line ships to hold the Blue Riband.

The new ship so impressed the German Kaiser, Wilhelm II, that he commented 'We must have some of these'. Carlisle and the Kaiser became friends and Carlisle visited the ex-head of state in exile after the end of World War 1 shortly before Carlisle's death. In terms of the design of the 'Olympic' class, Carlisle was responsible for the internal arrangements, decor and safety features. After the loss of the Titanic, he was one of the main expert witnesses at the British inquiry and outlined how he had advised installing 48 lifeboats on board the class and how 64 could

be accommodated using 16 pairs of davits. He died on 15 March 1926. Carlisle was related to Lord Pirrie by marriage; they were brothers-in-law.

Harold Cottam

The wireless operator on board the Carpathia, Cottam was aged 21 at the time of the disaster and, like other wireless operators, was a direct employee of the Marconi company rather than of Cunard or White Star. Born in Southwell, Nottinghamshire in 1891 he trained to be a wireless operator in London. He was paid £4 10s per month (plus board whilst on the ship) and his equipment on the Carpathia had a range of 250 miles.

He was the only qualified radio operator on board and had been on the point of retiring to bed, having been on duty since the early morning, when waiting for the Parisian to respond, he heard the Titanic's distress signal. Thereafter, after jointly informing Captain Rostron of the sinking, he remained in contact with the Titanic until the latter ceased transmissions. After the Carpathia had picked up survivors, Cottam was assisted in

relaying messages to and from shore by the surviving wireless operator from the Titanic, Harold Bride. After the tragedy, Cottam continued to work as a wireless operator until his retirement. He died on 30 May 1984.

Stanley Lord

Born on 13 January 1877, the captain of the Leyland Line-owned SS Californian, Stanley Lord – no relation of the author Walter Lord who wrote the classic account of the sinking in *A Night to Remember* – was one of the more controversial figures in the sinking of the Titanic as the Californian was sufficiently close to the sight of the tragedy to see the rockets being fired from the stricken ship; it was estimated that the two ships were less than 20 miles apart – indeed the subsequent US and British inquiries suggested that the two ships were in fact much closer – and members of the crew on board the Titanic were aware of the lights of another ship in the distance.

It was not until the morning of the 15th that Lord received a message from the Frankfurt that the Titanic had sunk and at 8.30am the Californian reached the site of the sinking. Following the arrival of the Californian in New York, Lord was interviewed by the US Inquiry on 26 April and, once back in Britain, he was also interviewed by the British Inquiry. The British Inquiry concluded that, had the Californian responded to the distress signals, the ship '... might have saved many if not all of the lives that were lost'. Although never convicted of any crime, Lord's reputation was undoubtedly sullied by the criticism and he spent much of the remainder of his life – particularly after publication in 1955 of *A Night to Remember* and the release of

the film based upon it (when he approached the Mercantile Marine Service association in Liverpool stating 'I am Lord of the Californian and I have come to clear my name.') – trying to restore his reputation.

He left the employment of Leyland Line – although whether he resigned or was dismissed is unclear – in August 1912 but then joined the Nitrate Producers Steamship Co the following year. He remained with the company until he resigned on health grounds in July 1928. Lord died on 24 January 1962 without knowing that his appeals made on his behalf by the MMSA's general secretary, Leslie Harrison, heard in 1965 and 1968 had failed. A quarter of a century later in 1992, the British Marine Accident Investigation Branch undertook a review of the evidence; the report issued following this review was equivocal as to the circumstances that pertained on the night of 14/15 April 1912.

RIGHT
John Pierpoint
Morgan.

John Pierpoint Morgan

One of the leading financiers of his generation, Morgan was a dominant figure in US business and a major collector of art, whose collection was to pass largely to the Metropolitan Museum of Art in New York following his death on 31 March 1913.

Born on 17 April 1837 in Hartford, Connecticut, he joined his father's banking business, in its London office, in 1856 before moving back to the USA the following year to work for Duncan, Shearman & Co. He rejoined his father's bank in 1860 and a long career in developing the business, which was, by 1900, one of the most powerful financial institutions in the world. Apart from his interest in banking, he was also heavily involved in the consolidation of the US railway and steel industries, creating the United States Steel Corporation in 1902, and in the formation of the General Electric Company in 1892 through the merger of Edison General Electric and the Thompson-Houston Electric Co.

Less well known, perhaps, was his involvement in the transatlantic shipping business and of the competition between shipping lines that led ultimately to the construction of the three 'Olympic' class liners. Competition between the shipping lines was fierce during the last decade of the 19th century, and profits for the shipping companies involved limited. In 1893, during a crossing of the Atlantic, Morgan was asked whether it was practical to try and buy up shipping lines in order to reduce competition and, thereby, encourage more realistic fares. Morgan's reply was that it ought to be, although it was not until later in the decade that he started to put this policy into practice when he acquired American Inman and Red

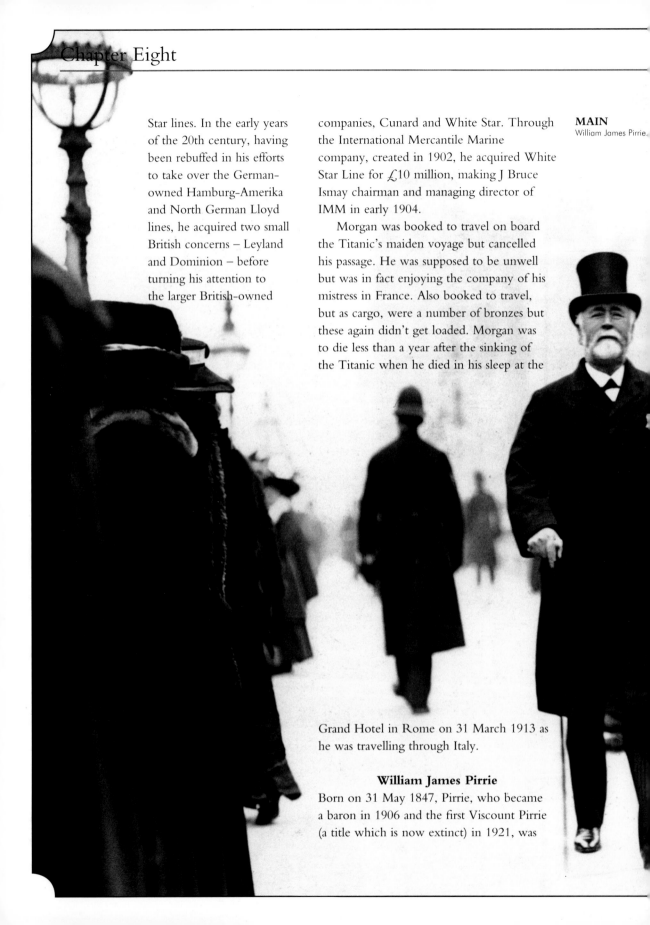

Star lines. In the early years of the 20th century, having been rebuffed in his efforts to take over the German-owned Hamburg-Amerika and North German Lloyd lines, he acquired two small British concerns – Leyland and Dominion – before turning his attention to the larger British-owned companies, Cunard and White Star. Through the International Mercantile Marine company, created in 1902, he acquired White Star Line for £10 million, making J Bruce Ismay chairman and managing director of IMM in early 1904.

Morgan was booked to travel on board the Titanic's maiden voyage but cancelled his passage. He was supposed to be unwell but was in fact enjoying the company of his mistress in France. Also booked to travel, but as cargo, were a number of bronzes but these again didn't get loaded. Morgan was to die less than a year after the sinking of the Titanic when he died in his sleep at the Grand Hotel in Rome on 31 March 1913 as he was travelling through Italy.

William James Pirrie

Born on 31 May 1847, Pirrie, who became a baron in 1906 and the first Viscount Pirrie (a title which is now extinct) in 1921, was

MAIN
William James Pirrie.

born in Quebec, in Canada, but came to
prominence as a businessman in Belfast
following his education at the city's Royal
Belfast Academical Institution. He joined
the newly-formed Harland & Wolff as a

gentleman apprentice in 1862 and became a partner in the business in 1874.

Following the death of Sir Edward Harland in 1895 he became chairman of the company but it was his backing of Morgan in the latter's struggle for control of White Star Line that swung the balance in favour of International Mercantile Marine over J Bruce Ismay. He was one of the three men – the others being Thomas Andrews and Ismay – that drew up the concept of the 'Olympic' class liners. Apart from his business activities, Pirrie was also active politically, serving as Lord Mayor of Belfast and as a member of the Northern Ireland Senate. He died on 6 June 1924 whilst on a business trip to South

America. Ironically, his body was returned to the UK on board the Olympic.

Arthur Henry Rostron

The captain of the Carpathia, Rostron's professionalism was a significant factor in the rescue of the survivors from the stricken ship. Born on 14 May 1869 just to the north of Bolton, Rostron joined the naval training ship HMS Conway at the age of 13 before being apprenticed to Messrs Williamson, Milligan & Co of Liverpool, who owned the Waverley Line.

He joined Cunard in January 1895 and was gradually promoted through the various officer ranks, achieving his first command, of the Pennonia, in 1911. Following a brief period serving with the Royal Naval Reserve, he returned to Cunard on 18 January 1912 to take command of the Carpathia. Following receipt of the distress signals, Rostron made for the stricken White Star ship as quickly as he could, exceeding the Carpathia's maximum speed of 14 knots by achieving 17 knots. Even so, the ship took three and a half hours to reach the site of the sinking and arrived in the early hours of the morning. Under Rostron's command, the Carpathia picked up more than 700 survivors before heading back to New York.

Following the sinking, Rostron gave evidence to both the US and UK inquiries and was presented with a silver cup by grateful survivors. After the sinking, Rostron continued his career with Cunard, becoming a Commander of the Order of the British Empire in 1919 and receiving his knighthood seven years later. In July 1928 Rostron became Commodore of the Cunard Line before retirement in 1931. He died on 4 November 1940.

LEFT
William James Pirrie accompanied by his wife on a business trip to South America on board the SS Arlanza. Pirrie died of pneumonia on the voyage.

RIGHT
Arthur Rostron.

Chapter Nine

The Titanic's Stores & Staffing

In order to provide sustenance for the more than 2,000 passengers and crew on board the Titanic for the transatlantic voyage, a vast amount of food was required. The following is a list of the foodstuffs loaded at Southampton prior to the maiden voyage:

Fresh meat	75,000lb
Fresh fish	11,000lb
Salted/dry fish	4,000lb
Bacon/ham	7,500lb
Poultry/game	25,000lb
Fresh eggs	40,000
Sausages	2,500lb
Potatoes	40 tons
Onions	3,500lb
Tomatoes	3,500lb
Fresh asparagus	800 bundles
Fresh green peas	2,500lb
Lettuce	8,000 heads
Sweetbreads	1,000
Ice cream	1,750qt
Coffee	2,200lb
Tea	800lb
Rice/dried beans	10,000lb
Sugar	10,000lb

LEFT
Artifacts from Titanic.

Flour	250 barrels
Apples	36,000
Oranges	36,000
Lemons	16,000
Grapes	1,000lb
Grapefruit	13,000
Marmalade/jam	1,120lb
Fresh milk	1,500gal
Fresh cream	2,400 pints
Condensed milk	600gal
Fresh butter	6,000lb
Ale/stout	15,000 bottles
Wines	1,000 bottles
Minerals	1,200 bottles
Cigars	8,000
Non-drinking water	664 tons
Drinking (fresh) water	792 tons

In order to serve this, the ship was also provided with:

57,600 pieces of crockery – these included 12,000 dinner plates, 4,500 breakfast saucers, 1,500 soufflé dishes, 4,500 soup bowls, 1,000 cream jugs and 1,200 pie dishes.

29,000 pieces of glassware – these included 2,000 wine glasses, 1,500 champagne glasses and 300 claret jugs.

44,000 items of cutlery – these included 1,500 fish knives, 1,500 fruit knives, 400 toast racks, 1,000 oyster forks, 100 grape scissors, 300 nutcrackers and 400 asparagus tongs.

196,100 items of linen – these included 4,000 aprons, 15,000 single sheets, 45,000 table napkins, 7,500 bath towels and 6,500 pantry towels.

Unlike other shipping companies, however, which branded cutlery and linen with the name of the ship, rather than of the line, White Star Line's cutlery, linen and crockery was not so treated, thereby making interchange between the various

ships operated by the company more straightforward. In order to allow the ship to function, the following were also required:

Water ballast 3,500 tons – this was required to trim the vessel to ensure an even keel whilst she was at sea although, despite this, the Titanic demonstrated a tendency to list slightly to port.

Coal c5,900 tons – the Titanic arrived at Southampton with 1,880 tons on board; she was estimated to have required to use some 415 tons whilst in Southampton generating steam to operate the cargo winches, heat and light. A further 4,427 tons were loaded in Southampton. The position was complicated by the fact that there was a coal strike in Britain at the time and supplies were short. The Titanic's supply had to be scraped together from a variety of sources. It had been estimated before the Titanic's maiden voyage that the ship would use some 720 tons of coal per day on her maiden voyage; the reality was some 100 tons less than that.

Apart from the stores required to operate the ship, the Titanic was also to carry cargo. The total cargo weighed some 559 tons, comprising some 11,500 items in all. The most unusual was, perhaps, a Renault car being shipped across the Atlantic by W E Carter, one of the first class passengers.

In order to function properly, the Titanic required a large crew. The major figures have already been described. Apart from the 69 members of staff employed in the Café Parisien, the Titanic also employed, amongst others, 62 second class stewards, 176 firemen, 106 saloon waiters and 30 greasers. Also on board were two doctors and a matron to man the ship's sick bay. The majority of crew members were allocated bunks on decks D, E, F and G. The total number of crew members on board was 892.

Chapter Ten

The Maiden Voyage

Following the arrival of the Titanic and the loading of the stores, the ship was scheduled to start her maiden voyage on Wednesday 10 April 1912. The crew started to arrive from 5.18am onwards, heading across the railway lines to enter the docks by Gate No 4 to join the Titanic, which was berthed at Berths 43 and 44. Captain Smith boarded at about 7.30am, heading straight for his cabin to be briefed by Chief Officer Wilde. Also boarding at 7.30am was Captain Maurice Harvey Clark

from the Board of Trade, who had already spent three days prior to the 10th inspecting the food supplies and other matters, and who was to clear the Titanic finally under the Merchant Shipping Acts. As part of his final inspection he got the crew to lower two of the starboard lifeboats to ensure that they functioned correctly and that the crew knew how to handle them. Having completed his inspections, Clark reported to Captain Smith on the bridge and also to Captain Benjamin Steele, White Star's marine superintendent.

Later in the morning the passengers started to arrive. The third class passengers, who boarded through the aft entrances on C deck, embarked between 9.30am and 11.00am. Following embarkation, the third class passengers underwent a medical examination. This was to differentiate them between 'steerage' – those passengers travelling at the lowest rate – and 'immigrants'. The medical examination was particularly rigorous for non-British citizens, many of whom were Scandinavians, as the US authorities could refuse entry to those deemed medically unfit.

At 11.30am the Boat Train, which had operated over the London & South Western main line from London Waterloo, arrived with the more select first and second class passengers; the passenger on board the train included Francis Browne. The first class passengers entered by way of gangways amidships to Deck B and were provided with guidebooks to the ship to enable them to get the most from their crossing. Stewards assisted both first and second class passengers to their cabins.

By the end of embarkation some 900 passengers had boarded the Titanic. By noon the great ship was ready to make her departure from Southampton; a small number

of crew members, who had been allowed additional time on shore (and who had visited local pubs as a result), failed to make it back to the ship in time. Ironically, their tardiness ensured that they survived. A number of replacement crew members, held on stand-by, took the place of those who had failed to arrive on time.

At 12 noon, with the Trinity House pilot, George Bowyer, on board the Blue Peter – the flag that indicated imminent departure – was raised on the foremast. The quartermaster, under instructions from Captain Smith, gave the first of three sharp blasts on the ship's whistle. Messages were relayed back from Wilde and Lightoller in the bow and from Murdoch and Pitman in the stern via Lowe on the bridge to Smith and Bowyer. With the lines from the same five tugs – Ajax, Hector, Hercules, Neptune and Vulcan – owned by Red Funnel that had assisted the ship to dock at Berth 44, the Titanic, not yet under her own power, was gently eased away from the dockside.

As the massive liner gradually emerged from her dock and clear of the harbour wall, the swell caused by her passage caused the SS New York, which had been moored alongside the Oceanic at Berth No 44, to break her moorings and to start to drift dangerously close to the Titanic. Fortunately, despite the strains, the moorings of the Oceanic held firm. The situation was rescued by prompt action on the part of Captain Gale on board the tug Vulcan, who at the second attempt managed to get a line aboard the New York and manoeuvre it away from danger. The two ships were no further than four feet apart when Gale's action saved the day.

The incident with the New York delayed the Titanic by about an hour. The liner now

set course for Cherbourg, where she was to pick up additional passengers. The French port was 77 nautical miles from Southampton and had been used by White Star Line as its French port for the transatlantic trade since 1907. The Titanic dropped anchor there at 6.30pm, still an hour behind schedule. Although Cherbourg was a deep water port, its inner harbour was not large enough to cope with vessels the size of the Olympic and Titanic. As a result, Harland & Wolff had also constructed two tenders to ferry passengers out from the harbour to the liners: the Traffic was built for third class passengers and the

MAIN
Tugged out of Southampton, Titanic would soon be on her way to Cherbourg

Nomadic was designed for first and second class travellers. The former was eventually sunk by a British torpedo on 17 January 1941 (having previously been scuttled as France fell in 1940 and then raised again by the Germans) whilst the Nomadic survived. After some years as a floating restaurant in Paris, the tender was purchased by the Northern Ireland Office to be repatriated to Belfast where the sole-surviving White Star Line-owned vessel is planned to form the centrepiece of a new exhibition devoted to Belfast, shipbuilding and the Titanic.

At Cherbourg, an additional 142 first class, 30 second and 102 third class

LEFT
Titanic departs
Queenstown, New
York bound.

passengers were waiting to board, whilst 15 first class and seven second class passengers waited to disembark. These cross-channel passengers had been charged £1 10s and £1 each respectively for their brief trip from Southampton. All of these had travelled from Paris on board the Train Transatlantique, which had taken some six hours to travel from Gare St Lazare and arrived for a scheduled embarkation of 4.00pm. The third class passengers were a mixed bag of travellers from the Balkans and Middle East. Amongst the first class passengers were Benjamin Guggenheim and Sir Cosmo and Lady Duff-Gordon. Once the passengers were aboard, the Titanic set course for its next port of call, Queenstown, County Cork in Ireland, at about 8.00pm. The ship reached Queenstown on the morning of 11 April. Shortly before the ship reached the Irish port, Captain Smith ordered an emergency drill. This tested the emergency doors and other safety equipment, although there is no record to indicate whether the lifeboats were again tested.

The Titanic reached its mooring point, about two miles offshore, at around 11.30am. As at Cherbourg, passengers were ferried to the ship by two tenders, but at Queenstown there was a further slight delay as the America and Ireland brought out the 120 first class, seven second class and 113 third class passengers. Also loaded were 1,385 bags of mail; the Titanic was a designated Royal Mail Ship (RMS) and part of her planned role was to ship mail to and from North America (there were five postal clerks – three American and two British – on board, whose task it was to sort the mail prior to arrival in the sorting room on the starboard side of Deck G). Seven passengers and one crew member also disembarked at Queenstown.

Amongst those disembarking at Queenstown was Francis Browne with his priceless collection of photographs.

Whilst the Titanic was at Queenstown, J Bruce Ismay – as he later admitted to the American inquiry – had a private conversation with the ship's chief engineer, Joseph Bell. According to the testimony Ismay gave in New York, 'It was our intention, if we had fine weather on Monday afternoon or Tuesday, to drive the ship at full speed... The Titanic, being a new ship, we were gradually working her up.' However, Ismay also admitted that he hadn't discussed the possibility of a high-speed run with Captain Smith. He later told the London inquiry that the Olympic had reached 22.75 knots and that he had hoped that the Titanic could have improved on that. The highest speed average achieved by a transatlantic liner was the 27.4 knots obtained by the Mauretania in 1907 when becoming the holder of the Blue Riband. Such a speed was well beyond the capabilities of the Titanic and so the theory, reported by a number of survivors, that Smith was endeavouring to beat the record is unlikely. However, that the ship was being put through its paces is undeniable. The ship's speed increased each day and, on Sunday 14 April, the last three of the 24 main boilers were lit bringing the ship's speed up to 22.5 knots. If all had gone according to plan, the five auxiliary boilers would have been lit on Monday 15 April to see if the ship could match, fully loaded, the 23.5 knots she had achieved when lightly loaded between Southampton and Cherbourg.

Following the transfer of passengers and mail, the Titanic weighed anchor at about 1.30pm and headed off passed the Daunt lightship, where the pilot was dropped before heading towards the Atlantic. One of the steerage passengers – Eugene Daly – had brought his bagpipes on board and as Ireland slipped astern he played the tune *Erin's Lament*. In setting his course for the trip across the Atlantic Captain Smith had a number of options. He selected the Autumn Southern Track rather than, for the time of year, more usual Outward Southern Track. The former had the advantage of being the shorter route but, by being 60 miles north of the latter, also meant that the ship was close to any likely ice. In selecting the Autumn Southern Track, Smith was running counter to company policy – which dictated that the southern route should be taken between mid-December and mid-March (although, given that it was now April, Smith was probably justified in his decision) – and it was not uncommon for liners to seek to take

advantage of the shorter route in order to post impressive crossing times. However, the winter of 1911/12 had proved to be milder than most, with the result that the Arctic ice sheet was breaking up more rapidly than usual and icebergs had been drifting south into the shipping lanes, indeed as far south as Bermuda. Captain Smith was aware of the presence of ice as the trade press had been reporting it in the months preceding Titanic's maiden voyage.

During the ship's first 24 hours at sea – from noon on Thursday 11 April through to noon on Friday 12 April – everything seemed to be progressing well and some 386 nautical miles were covered during this period. In the wireless room Jack Phillips and Harold Bride were busy taking and receiving messages on behalf of passengers whilst also receiving messages from other ships regarding

BELOW
Passengers enjoyed the luxuries that were on offer, including the Smoke Room.

navigational conditions. By lunchtime on 12 April, the Titanic had received five messages from other ships ahead of it warning of ice and these were followed by a further four – from the Avala, the East Point, the Californian and the Manitou – later in the day. The ice was, however, still far ahead of the ship and so the ship made more rapid progress on the succeeding two days – achieving 519 nautical miles by noon on the 13th and a further 546 nautical miles by noon on Sunday the 14th – as the new engines were gradually put through their paces.

On the morning of Sunday 14 April, which had dawned cold and clear but with a slight haze, the first of the day's sequence of ice warnings was received, when at 9.00am the captain of the Caronia sent the Titanic a message that westbound steamers were encountering ice. Captain Smith acknowledged the message and the information was recorded in the chart room. Under White Star regulations, a lifeboat drill should have been held during the morning

of the Sunday; however, these were not popular with the crew and, in light of the cold weather, it was decided not to hold the practice. As it was a Sunday, a religious service was, however, held.

At 1.42pm a further warning of ice was received, this time from the Baltic; whilst the message was acknowledged by Captain Smith, he appears not to have been on the bridge at the time – it was the middle of the serving of lunch – and none of the three surviving bridge officers recalled receiving it when pressed at the two inquiries. It would appear that Captain Smith passed the warning on to J Bruce Ismay in order to alert him to the presence of ice and that, inexplicably, Ismay held on to the message until the early evening. During the course of the afternoon, further warnings of ice were received but the ship's direction did not change until 5.50pm, when the planned change of course from S62°W to S86°W at the 'Corner' took place.

Whilst the ship headed westwards, the Titanic's passengers were enjoying the facilities that the ship offered. Apart from the orchestra, the crew did not lay on activities for the passengers in the belief that the ship was well provided with options to entertain the passengers. Thus, during the course of the Sunday, it would have been possible to see passengers reading books in the libraries (Colonel Gracie, for example, was reading *Old Dominion*, written by Mary Johnston which was a book of adventure and escape stories), making use of the swimming pool, gymnasium and Turkish baths, playing cards, walking on the promenade deck and playing deck games. However, passengers did note that the ambient temperature on deck was getting colder and at least commented that this drop in temperature was indicative perhaps of the presence of ice. Later in the evening, again reflecting the fact that it was a Sunday, some 100 passengers gathered in the second class dining saloon for a service hymn singing organised by the Reverend E C Carter; this concluded at around 10.30pm.

At 6.00pm Lightoller returned to the bridge to start his next four-hour watch, taking over from Wilde. Lightoller noted that the ship was sailing at 21.5 knots on a heading of S86°W true. At 7.30pm he took an accurate measurement of the ship's position using his sextant, which he passed to Boxhall for the actual calculation. Contrary to standing orders, Captain Smith was not on the bridge at this time but was attending a private party, hosted by the Wideners, in the à la carte restaurant. Amongst other guests at the party were other first class travellers including the Thayers and Carters. The Captain left the Wideners' party at about 8.55pm and returned to the bridge. During the course of the evening, whilst Captain Smith had been at the party, Lightoller

had been noting the gradual dropping of the outside temperature; by the time that Smith returned to the bridge at 9.00pm, the outside temperature had dropped to 33°F (1°C). The rapidly dropping temperature was an indication of the presence of icebergs and Lightoller had already noted in the night order book the necessity of keeping a sharp look out for icebergs. According to Lightoller's calculations, based on the warnings he had seen, it was likely that ice would be encountered from about 11.30pm although other bridge officers had calculated a slightly earlier time.

At 8.00pm Archie Jewel and George Symons took over as look-outs in the crow's nest from George Hogg and Frank Evans. Also at this time Boxhall and Moody came on duty, both of them regularly checking the air and water temperatures. The sea was calm and, despite the lack of a moon, the stars were clear; when Captain Smith returned to the bridge, he and Lightoller had a conversation about the weather conditions and about the visibility of icebergs in such climatic conditions. The calm water meant,

BELOW
Binoculars retrieved from Titanic.

BELOW
A telephone from
Titanic, perhaps
used by Fleet calling
the bridge.

for example, that one of the indications of the presence of icebergs was the sea water rippling around them; clearly, in completely calm conditions, this could not occur.

In the crow's nest the look-outs kept a wary eye out for ice. White Star Line was unusual at the time in that it would only employ look-outs who had gone to the expense of having an eye test. They were also, in theory, provided with a pair of binoculars, which were notionally in the charge of the Second Officer but which were stored in a specially-built cupboard in the crow's nest itself. In terms of the actual provision of binoculars in the crow's nest on the Titanic, there is some element of doubt. When the original Second Officer, David Blair, was replaced, he took with him the keys to the cupboard in the crow's nest but left his binoculars – White Star Line issued binoculars to each ship's officers stamped with their rank and, until 1895, issued them separately to the crow's nest; after that date, the issuing of binoculars to the crow's nest was left at the captain's discretion – and during the crossing from Southampton to

Cherbourg the look-outs reported the fact that none had been issued to them although they had had them during the trip from Belfast to Southampton. Both Murdoch and Wilde were made aware of this omission but George Hogg later reported 'I had them from Belfast to Southampton but from Southampton to where the accident occurred we never had them.' However, a pair of binoculars was located within the debris field at a point consistent with them falling from the crow's nest as the ship finally broke up.

Having returned to the bridge, Captain Smith retired to his cabin at about 9.30pm having issued instructions to Lightoller that he was to be roused immediately if anything untoward occurred although it appears that Lightoller omitted to relay the message to Murdoch when the latter came on duty at 10.00pm. At 9.40pm a further message, this time from the Mesaba was received warning of ice in the area of Longitude 49°W to 50°30'W; as the Titanic was approaching Longitude 49°W, this ice lay directly ahead of the ship. Unfortunately, the message was not passed directly from the wireless room as the wireless operators were engaged in handing transmissions to and from passengers – the business from which Marconi derived its income.

At 10.00pm, there was a further change of watch, with Murdoch replacing Lightoller on the bridge and with Fred Fleet (concentrating on the port side) and Reginald Lee (concentrating on the starboard) taking over in the crow's nest 50 feet above the forecastle. At 10.30pm the Titanic passed the Rappahannock with the latter sending a further warning of the presence of ice; although the message was acknowledged, there was no reduction in the ship's speed, which was still around 22 knots, nor in the course that the ship was sailing.

Around 11.00pm, according to the look-outs, the previously clear night developed a slight haze and, at 11.15pm, Fleet grabbed the warning bell and gave it three pulls in order to alert the bridge of an obstruction ahead. He then tried calling the bridge using the telephone but could not elicit an immediate response. According to the statement he made later to the British inquiry, Fleet had spotted 'A black object, high above the water, dead ahead.' At this stage, the iceberg was about 10 or 11 miles ahead. Fleet tried to raise the bridge – both by use of the bell and the telephone – on several occasions but it took several attempts to get through and, even when the message was relayed, the look-outs noticed no change of course or speed. Eventually Fleet had a conversation with Moody that conveyed the urgency of the situation, reporting to the officer that he had seen an 'Iceberg right ahead'. This was acknowledged by Moody and reported to Murdoch; Fleet noticed an almost immediate turn to port.

Murdoch himself, standing on the open wing of the bridge, saw the iceberg on the starboard side at a distance of some 800 yards. Returning to the bridge he ordered the ship to turn 'hard a–a starboard' whilst also using the engine room telegraph to instruct the engineers to 'Stop: Full Speed Astern' (when the Titanic was given its one-day sea trial earlier in the month, the emergency stop had required 850 yards even when travelling at a lower speed than that on the evening of 14 April; with Murdoch taking action with the ship some 800 yards away it was inevitable that the ship would strike the object – the big question was how severely).

Some 39 seconds after Fleet's conversation with Moody, the ship struck the iceberg; there was contact for about 10 seconds as the berg scraped along the starboard side of the ship – 10 seconds that would lead to more than 1,500 passengers and crew losing their lives in the icy waters of the North Atlantic.

LEFT
Captain Smith had retired to his cabin prior to the disaster.

RIGHT
Latitude 41' 46N
and longitude
50' 14W, the
place where the
Titanic sank.

Chapter Eleven

The Final Moments

Between the collision with the iceberg at 11.40pm and the Titanic actually sinking at 2.20am, there was more than two and a half hours of activity, some of it frenetic and some less so. Many of those on board evinced considerable courage whilst the behaviour of others was perhaps less commendable.

Most passengers were unaware of the collision and those that did feel the impact commented on how slight it felt. Jack Thayer commented, for example, 'If I had a brimful glass of water in my hand not a drop would have been spilled.' Mrs Astor initially thought that it was some mishap in the kitchen, whilst J Bruce Ismay was awakened by what he thought was the loss of a propeller.

One of the passengers in the first class smoking room, Hugh Woolner, noted '… a sort of stopping, a sort – not exactly shock, but a sort of slowing down. And then we felt a rip that gave a sort of slight twist to the whole room. Everybody, so far as I could see, stood up and a number of men walked out rapidly through the swinging doors on the port side and ran along to the rail that was behind the mast.' The journalist William Stead was on deck when the collision happened and both he and his companion,

Father Thomas Byles, thought that little of note had happened.

The reality, however, was that below the water line, a gash some 300 feet in length had been scored some 15 feet above the keel. It has subsequently been estimated that the total area exposed to water flooding in was no more than 12 square feet, but this was over a considerable distance, with the result that sea water started to enter the forepeak tank, holds 1, 2 and 3, and the forward boiler room (No 6). The ship could remain afloat provided that only two of the watertight compartments were flooded, but the damage caused by the collision caused the bow section to lower in the water, thereby causing the water level to rise above the bulkheads separating the watertight compartments. Of the bulkheads, only the first, nearest the bow, extended up to deck C, bulkheads two and 11-15 extended to deck D, but those from three to 10 extended only to deck E. With the water reaching boiler room No 6 and with the bow section settling deeper in the water, the level of water on board was rising above deck E. The ship's predicament was outlined to Captain Smith by Thomas Andrews when the two of them made a 10 minute inspection of the damage. As the ship's designer he was acutely aware

LEFT
An artist's
impression of
Captain Smith
issuing his 'Last
Orders'.

that the water entering into more than two of the ship's watertight compartments meant that the vessel was effectively doomed. By 12.30am, some 16,000 tons of water had already entered the ship and, with the level already rising above deck E, the Titanic was inevitably destined to sink.

Following the collision, Captain Smith returned to the bridge enquiring 'What have we struck, Mr Murdoch'. Murdoch replied 'An iceberg sir. I hard-a-starboarded and reversed the engines and I was going to hard-a-port around it, but she was too close. I could not do any more.' Smith then asked Murdoch 'Have you closed the watertight doors?', to which Murdoch replied in the affirmative. As the duty officers arrived on the bridge, they were given tasks; curiously, however the off-duty officers (such as Lowe who was awakened by the commotion outside his cabin on the boat deck at 12.45am) weren't roused to assist in organising the passengers and crew. Boxhall, for example, was sent down below to inspect the damage; he reported back 15 minutes later to report that he found no damage above deck F but that a postal clerk had informed him of water entering A deck G level. On his return, shortly after midnight, Boxhall was instructed to calculate the ship's position, which he did using the position calculated by Lightoller from the stars at 7.30pm. This was the notorious 41°46'N/50°14'W; the inaccuracy could have been caused by a number of factors and is probably explicable under the circumstances in which Boxhall was operating. Factors that might have caused error included overestimating the ship's speed by half a knot – 22 knots as opposed to the actual speed of 21.5 – the subtle changes required

to the ship's clock during the period from 7.30pm onwards and the one-knot southerly current through which the Titanic was passing. Whatever the cause, the erroneous information was soon being transmitted by Jack Phillips and Harold Bride from the wireless room as they started to issue 'CQD' messages at around 12.15am.

Amongst the ships in the area was the RMS Carpathia. On board, the ship's wireless operator, Harold Cottam, was waiting for a reply to a message that he'd sent earlier to the Parisian. Cottam had been on duty since 7.00am and he was eager for bed. Whilst waiting for the Parisian to respond, he listened in to other transmissions from Cape Cod; becoming aware that the shore station had a number of signals for the Titanic, Cottam finally made contact with the White Star Line vessel, sending the message 'I say, old man, do you know there is a batch of messages coming through for you from MCC [Cape Cod]'. Phillips responded immediately with 'CQD' to which Cottam replied 'Shall I tell my captain? Do you require assistance?' Phillips again responded 'Yes. Come quick.' Cottam took immediate action; he and the Carpathia's officer of the watch, H V Dean, roused the ship's captain and alerted him to the situation. Captain Rostron on board the Carpathia responded to the unfolding tragedy with alacrity and, in a masterful display of seamanship, set course for the Titanic's reported position. He undoubtedly was one of the heroes of the night.

Shortly before midnight, J Bruce Ismay came up to the bridge – his first visit there since the voyage began – to be briefed on the ship's condition by Captain Smith. Smith reported that the ship was badly damaged and that she was taking in water at the forepeak

LEFT

Lowering the first lifeboats.

and in four of the watertight compartments. Shortly after midnight, Smith ordered Wilde to uncover the lifeboats and Murdoch began to muster the passengers. Wilde was assisted in his task by one of the look-out, George Symons. Lightoller was then given permission by the captain to swing the boats out and, at 12.25am, the order was given to start loading them, women and children first.

Below decks, the situation was fast deteriorating. In boiler room No 5, the crew had managed to get the pumps working and were winning the battle to keep the water level down. However, the pressure in the boilers was rising rapidly, causing the safety valves to blow off and there was a danger that the steam pipes might burst. Just as the order was given to draw the fire, the damaged bulkhead between boiler rooms five and six collapsed, with water rushing in.

Lightoller initially intended to load the lifeboats from A deck and, having ordered the women and children to that level, lowered the first lifeboat (No 4) at about 12.45am. However, the windows on the forward section of A deck were locked and, rather than return the boat to the boat deck and load it from there, Lightoller elected to try and find the key.

Shortly after the order to uncover the lifeboats, Boxhall was instructed to start firing the ship's distress rockets. Manufactured by the Cotton Powder Co Ltd, the rockets – 'socket signals' – were designed to reach a height of 800 feet. A total of 24 of these rockets were brought to the bridge by Rowe and by Quartermaster Alfred Olliver, with the first being launched at around 12.45am. The launching of the first rocket occurred contemporaneously with the launching of the first lifeboat, No 7, and with preparation for launching lifeboat No 3. Aware that the situation might get out of hand, Lowe, who had been roused at 12.45am, returned to his cabin in order to arm himself prior to heading back to the boat deck to assist with the loading of the lifeboats.

Given the fact that the Sunday morning lifeboat drill had been cancelled and that the only testing of the lifeboats had been the brief trial undertaken at Southampton, it is perhaps of little surprise that the launching of the lifeboats proved problematic. Although the instruction has gone out for women and children to be put in the lifeboats, a certain number of male passengers had boarded the early lifeboats to have been launched; male crew members, however, were supposed to have been on board as they were required to row the lifeboats away from the sinking ship and to maintain order on board them. The chaotic launchings meant not only were many of the scarce lifeboats lowered with many fewer than the permitted number of passengers on board but a number also lacked the requisite crew members to handle the boats correctly once in the water. Such was the case with lifeboat No 6; this was launched at 1.00am with only two crew members on board along with 25 women passengers. As no additional crew members could be allocated, Lightoller permitted a male passenger, Arthur Peuchen (who claimed to have some knowledge of yachting), to board and much of rowing of the boat was undertaken ultimately by the women passengers led by the indomitable Mrs Molly Brown.

The launching of No 6 had been preceded by a few minutes by the launching of No 5, which was also only partially filled. Some 30 women and children were on board but no further could be found; as a result, Third Officer Herbert Pitman, in charge of the boat allowed four male passengers to board. A total of 39 were on board when No 5 was finally lowered to the water. As the boat was lowered, two further male passengers leapt on board, one of them injuring Mrs Annie May Stengel, a first class passenger, as he landed on her. Only 25 women and children could be found for the next lifeboat, No 3, with the result that 10 male passengers as well as 15 crew members were therefore allowed to board.

Of the lifeboats fitted to the Titanic, two – Nos 1 on the starboard side and 2 on the port – were considered emergency boats and were always kept at a state of heightened readiness. They were, however, smaller (at 25 feet rather than the 30 feet of the remainder) and had a smaller capacity (40 as opposed to 60) than the remainder of the lifeboats. It was adjacent to lifeboat No 1 that Sir Cosmo Duff-Gordon, his wife, her secretary and two others had gathered. Duff-Gordon enquired of Murdoch and Lowe as to whether the five could board the boat. The officers acquiesced and the five, along with seven members of crew including the look out George Symons, boarded. The boat was lowered with only these 12 on board. The fact that Duff-Gordon was to survive when a number of equally prominent male passengers had not was to result in a certain amount of opprobrium when he returned to Britain although he was exonerated by the subsequent inquiry, claiming that when he and his party were permitted to board the boat that no other women and children were present.

Also being prepared at about the same time as lifeboat No 1 was No 8, the boarding of which was being supervised by Lightoller.

It was on this boat that Mrs Ida Straus was initially placed; however, Lightoller's refusal to allow her husband, Isador, to join her meant that she disembarked. Their maid, Ellen Bird, was however, to escape on board No 8. A group of some 30 third class passengers, women and children, were brought up but few were permitted to board; again, it was symptomatic of the problems in handling the lifeboats that allocation of berths seems to have been class based with many of the steerage passengers effectively abandoned to their fate. Lifeboat No 8 was eventually launched with 24 passengers and four members of crew on board. The passengers on board No 8 included Lucy-Noel Martha, Countess of Rothes. The next lifeboat to be launched was No 9, which was better filled, with a total of 56 on board. This was followed by No 11 with some 70 in total; this was the first boat to be launched with more than the maximum number of bodies on board.

The next lifeboat to be launched was No 10; by this stage the ship was developing a more pronounced list to port and a number of passengers were sent to the starboard side in order to try and reduce this list. Lifeboat No 10 was lowered with 55 passengers (including two stowaways – a Japanese and an Armenian – aboard). As the boat was lowered, a 56th passenger – described as a 'crazed Italian' – leapt aboard. Following this, No 12 was the next to be handled with 40 women and children from second and steerage classes on board plus two crewmen – John Poigndestre and Fred Clench – and one first class passenger. By this stage, discipline was starting to slip and, before the boat was lowered, Poigndestre and Lightoller had to prevent other passengers attempting to rush the boat.

By the time Lowe and Wilde moved on to the next boat to be loaded, No 14, the situation had deteriorated further and passengers again tried to board without permission. According to Joseph Scarrott, one of the crew members working on No 14, Lowe – who had earlier retrieved his pistol – threatened to shoot any passengers who caused trouble. One passenger – a teenage boy – on board the lifeboat was ordered by Lowe to return to the stricken ship. With 64 on board, including himself, Lowe ordered the boat to be lowered, firing three shots to deter any last minute attempts to leap on board. As the lifeboat descended, a problem developed with the davits with the result that Lowe had to release the boat using the release gear, causing the boat to drop five feet into the water. This resulted in the boat springing a leak that required to be baled out until the passengers were rescued by the Carpathia.

The next lifeboat into the water was No 16 with 56 passengers and crew on board; simultaneously with the lowering of No 16 on the port side, No 13 was being lowered on the starboard. As the lifeboat was lowered, Lawrence Beesley, who had been invited to board by a crew member, noticed what he believed to be the last distress rocket fired from the ship. Unfortunately, again as a result presumably of lack of training amongst the crew, when No 13 hit the water, no-one on board was aware as to how to release the boat with the result that it drifted towards the stern and was in danger of being crushed by lifeboat No 15 being lowered at that time. Fortunately, shouts from below were heard and the lowering of No 15 ceased whilst No 13 was released. No 15 was eventually lowered with 14 crew members, one first

class passenger and 53 women from third class, making a total of 68 in all.

On the starboard side, attention now switched to collapsible C, which Murdoch had positioned under the davits used for lifeboat No 3. Six crew members, under the

BELOW
Survivors in a
crowded lifeboat.

command of Quartermaster Rowe, were allocated to the boat. As order continued to deteriorate, Murdoch was forced to fire his pistol into the air to clear the boat of 'Italians and foreigners who had sneaked into it'; just as third class passengers were discriminated against, so too were non-British or US citizens. For example, the staff of the à la carte restaurant Café Parisien, being largely Italian and neither passengers nor crew, were effectively barred from making their way to the boat deck and thus perished. Luigi Gatti's

BELOW Survivors in a crowded lifeboat.

secretary, Paul Mauge, however, was to survive; a fact that he attributed to the British inquiry as it was because he was dressed like a passenger. A total of 39 passengers and crew were loaded on board collapsible C, although it was actually designed to hold 47. Amongst those that made good their escape on this boat was J Bruce Ismay. Again to prevent any last-minute attempts to leap aboard, shots were fired.

Lightoller's attention was now focused on lifeboat No 2. He discovered it was full of 'dagoes' who he ordered off at gunpoint. He then ordered three crew members and Boxhall to board and a total of 21 passengers were then allowed on, making a total of 25 – again well below the boat's actual capacity of 40. With No 2 launched, Lightoller returned to lifeboat No 4, which had earlier been held up as a result of the locked windows on deck A. After some confusion, with the intended passengers being switched from deck to deck, the windows on deck A had been opened. However, with the ship's increasing list to

port, there was now a considerable distance between the deck and the lifeboat. In order to bring the boat closer to the deck, boat hooks were used and the boat lashed to the side of the liner. A makeshift ladder was then used to allow passengers and crew to board.

Amongst the passengers waiting patiently to board lifeboat No 4 were the Astors, Thayers, Wideners and Ryersons. Initially, Lightoller refused permission for 13-year-old Jack Ryerson to board the boat with his mother – it was reported that John Jacob Astor placed a woman's hat on the boy and told him 'There, now you're a girl and you can go' (although this may be apocryphal as Mrs Ryerson did not mention the statement in her affidavit later) – but was overruled by the rest of the group. Despite the fact that the boat was still less than full, the men were prevented from entering the boat, despite requests from Astor, for example, that he be allowed to join his pregnant wife. Lifeboat No 4 was lowered at 1.55am with Astor and the other men waving farewell to their wives

MAIN
Lifeboats surround
the sinking Titanic.

and reassuring them that they would be on another boat. Following the launch of No 4, Astor descended to the ship's kennels on deck F, in order to release his Airedale terrier, Kitty, and the others that had been kennelled there for the duration of the voyage.

Whilst there was feverish activity on the boat deck, in the wireless room the two Marconi operators, Jack Phillips and Harold Bride, were hard at work sending out distress messages; initially these used the tradition 'CQD' code favoured by British mariners but later Phillips switched to the recently introduced 'SOS'. As the ship's generator gradually failed, so the signals issued by the Titanic got gradually fainter and fainter. Shortly after 2.00am, Captain Smith came to the wireless room and relieved Phillips and Bride of their duties; they had done as much as they could and, with the ship's power failing and the water rapidly rising, they could achieve no more. As Phillips made to pick up his life jacket, it was seized by another crew member. In the altercation that followed, Bride and Phillips knocked out the perpetrator and reclaimed the life jacket. There is some doubt as to the actual fate of Phillips, although the fact that he did not survive the sinking is known. Bride, however, did survive and was one of those ultimately rescued from collapsible B.

Back on the boat deck, Lightoller was organising the loading of collapsible boat D. When this was lowered at 2.05am, there were 37 women and children on board, mostly third class, as well as three members of crew. Although Lightoller had attempted to prevent any men, other than crewmen, boarding, one third class passenger – Joseph Duegmin – had smuggled himself on board and, as the boat was lowered, two more men

– Hokan Bjornstron Steffanson and Hugh Woolner – leapt on board. A third man, Frederick Hoyt (whose wife was already on board the boat), also jumped but missed the boat and had to be plucked from the sea. Collapsible D, with a capacity of 47, departed – the final boat launched from the davits – with 44 crew and passengers on board.

With the bulk of the lifeboats now launched – only collapsibles A and B located on the roof of the deckhouse remained – those on board the ship were effectively resigned to their fate. In the first class smoking room a group of passengers – Archie Butt, Francis D Millet, Clarence Moore and Arthur Ryerson – played cards and had a final drink before heading out on deck. The Titanic's designer, Thomas Andrews, was last spotted in the same room staring at the painting over the fireplace in the same room. At the stern of the stricken vessel Father Thomas Byles was offering confession whilst Wallace Hartley and the orchestra, having played more popular music to this point, switched to the playing of hymns.

Elsewhere, as the water gradually encroached upon the boat deck a number of the ships officers and men – Wilde, Murdoch, Lightoller and Moody amongst them – were struggling to release collapsible boats A and B. The former had been snagged in the rigging and so attention was switched to the latter. There is some uncertainty as to how collapsible A reached the water – contradictory evidence was given subsequently – but it did find its way into the water the correct way up. Unfortunately, during the process, the sides of the boat collapsed and, of those who tried to get aboard the boat whilst it was semi-flooded only 14 were to survive to be rescued. As the rising water rushed over the roof, collapsible lifeboat B was washed overboard and ended up in the sea upside down.

By now the ship was in its death throes, with some 1,500 passengers and crew still on board. There was inevitably increasing panic, particularly amongst those from third class who had only just made their escape on to deck. By this stage both Lightoller and Bride had entered the water, with the latter under the upturned collapsible B. Other passengers, such as Archibald Gracie and 17-year-old Jack Thayer – who had been separated from his parents earlier – also decided to take their chances in the water. Thayer swam strongly until he was some 40 yards from the ship he then looked at the ship. He commented later 'The ship seemed to be surrounded with a glare and stood out of the night as though she were on fire'. Another witness to the final sinking, Mrs Charlotte Collyer in lifeboat No 14, recalled that the ship resembled 'an enormous glow worm, for she was alight from the rising waterline, clear to her stern… electric lights blazing in every cabin, lights on all decks, and lights on her mastheads.' With the ship's generators still producing electricity, lights were even visible from those cabins now under water, giving the sea a peculiar luminescence.

Whilst the onlookers watched, the forward funnel, already partially submerged, broke away with a minor explosion. The second funnel was also now partially inundated as those on the lifeboats heard explosions from within the ship. Finally, just after 2.15am, the ship's generators finally gave way, plunging the ship and all those around it into darkness. With the ship now virtually vertical in the water, the Titanic finally sank at 2.20am. At the time there was some debate as to whether the ship's back was broken before she actually sank. According to Jack Thayer, who had by now boarded the upturned collapsible B in the company of Lightoller, 'The ship did not break in two and could not be broken in two. The ship was at 60° when the lights went out, but the stern continued to rise until it was vertical.' Lightoller, Lowe and Pitman were also of the opinion that the ship sank intact although their view was contradicted by a number of surviving crew members who expressed a belief that the ship had broken up prior to sinking although they couldn't agree on the point where the ship did actually break its back.

At the time it was impossible to verify the nature of the actual sinking; it took the discovery of the wreck more than 70 years later to confirm that the ship had, indeed, broken up as she sank.

With the ship sunk, the survivors on board the various lifeboats were left awaiting rescue. Fifth Officer Harold Lowe gathered together a number of lifeboats – Nos 4, 10, 12 and 14 as well as collapsible D – and, by redistributing the survivors between the various boats, he cleared No 14 of all except a small crew. It was his intention to return to the site of the sinking to pick up survivors; however, it was to be an hour before he was able to make the return and, by that time, most of those in the water had died. He was, however, to pluck five from the freezing water alive, although one of these, a steward, subsequently died. It was going to be a long and cold night until the rockets from the Carpathia were spotted just before dawn. As the sun started to rise over the eastern horizon, the Carpathia came into view and, at 4.10am, the first of the survivors were taken on board.

RIGHT
Illustration of the imagined fate of the Titanic, lying on the sea bed with an iceberg.

Chapter Twelve

Titanic Timeline

Warnings to Rescue – (Note on timings: crews on each ship adjusted their clocks as their vessels headed east or west to reflect the changing time of the zones through which they were operating. During the period between 8pm and midnight, the clocks on the Titanic would have been set back by about 23 minutes. The following schedule is based upon the timings generally recorded in print subsequent to the sinking.)

9.00am – Captain Barr of the Caronia sent a radio message to the Titanic: 'Captain, Titanic – Westbound steamers report bergs, growlers and field ice in 42° to 51°W, 12th April. Compliments – Barr'. The message was received by Captain Smith and acknowledged by him. At the time, the ship was 100 miles north and 30 miles east of the position quoted. The position of the ice was noted in the chart room. This message would appear to be the only one that was received by the bridge.

1.42pm – The SS Baltic sent a radio message to the Titanic: 'Captain Smith, Titanic – Have had moderate variable winds and clear, fine weather since leaving. Greek steam Athenia reports passing icebergs and large quantities of field ice today in lat 41° 51'N, Long 49° 52'W.... Wish you and Titanic all success – Commander.' At this stage the Titanic was 45 miles north and 180 miles east of the ice but was closing on the location at 22 knots. The message was passed to Captain Smith, who acknowledged it, but it does not appear to have been passed to the officer of the watch. At the subsequent inquiry, it was reported by one of the surviving officers that the information about ice failed to reach the bridge and was thus not plotted on the ship's charts. At this time the Titanic was at 42°35'N/45°50'W.

1.45pm – A warning was issued by the SS Amerika that icebergs lay south of the Titanic's intended route; however, as the warning had been issued to the US Hydrographic Department, the message wasn't relayed to the bridge.

5.50pm – The Titanic altered course from S62°W to S86°W. This was the 'Corner', the point at 42°N latitude, which, according to the sailing order, the Titanic was to cross the 47°W longitude.

6.00pm – Lightoller returned to the bridge to start his four-hour watch replacing Chief Officer Wilde. He noted that the ship was sailing at 'full ahead' on a course of S86°W true.

6.30pm – apparent ship's time; lat 42° 3'N, long 49° 9'W. Three large bergs five miles to southwards of us. Regards – Lord.' Bride subsequently claimed that he'd taken the message to the bridge but none of the surviving officers could recall this.

7.00pm – The outside air temperature was 43°F. The three extra boilers lit during the morning were connected to the engines;

this gave the ship an extra knot of speed if required.

7.15pm – Lamp Trimmer Samuel Hemmings reported to the bridge that all the ship's navigation lights were in place. First Officer Murdoch ordered him to close the forescuttle hatch, commenting 'as we are in the vicinity of ice and there is a glow coming from that and I want everything dark before the bridge.'

7.30pm – Harold Bride in the wireless room on the Titanic intercepts a message from the Californian to another Leyland-owned vessel SS Antillian: 'The Captain, Antillian: 6.30pm apparent ship's time; lat 42°3'N, long 49°9'W. Three large bergs five miles to southward of us. Regards – Lord'. The outside air temperature had dropped to 39°F; the rapidly dropping temperature was evidence of the potential presence of ice. On the bridge Lightoller took a star sight with his sextant in order to ascertain the ship's position. It was this reading that would later be used to estimate the ship's position when issuing the distress messages over the wireless.

8.00pm – Archie Jewel and George Symons replaced George Hogg and Frank Evans as look-outs. Boxhall and Moody came on duty on the bridge.

8.10pm – Lightoller ordered the ship's Quartermaster, Hitchens, to order the ship's carpenter, J Maxwell, to check the water on board the ship as he was concerned about it freezing. He also passed the message, via Maxwell, to Joseph Bell, the chief engineer, to check the fresh water that was designed for use in the boilers. This was stored in the ship's double hull and Lightoller's request suggests that he was concerned that the sea temperature, as well as the air temperature, might drop below freeing.

8.30pm – A hymn singing session, attended by more than 100 passengers, commenced in the second class dining room; it would continue until after 10.00pm.

8.55pm – Captain Smith, who had been dining in the à la carte restaurant at a private party hosted by Harry Widener, left the party and returned briefly to the bridge and engaged Lightoller in conversation. He retired to bed at about 9.20pm telling Lightoller 'If it becomes at all doubtful let me know at once; I'll be just inside'.

9.30pm – With Jack Phillips and Harold Bride in the radio room a further report of large icebergs in the liner's route was received from the Mesaba – 'To Titanic and eastbound ships: Ice report in latitude 42N, to 41.25N, longitude 49W, to 50.30W. Saw much heavy pack ice and great number large icebergs. Also field ice. Weather good, clear.' – but again this wasn't passed on to the bridge.

9.40pm – A further wireless warning was received from Stanley Howard Adams on board the Mesaba: From Mesaba to Titanic. In Latitude 42°N to 41° 25'N, Longitude 49° to Long 50° 30'W. Saw much heavy pack ice and great numbers large icebergs, also field ice. Weather good, clear.' Bride retired from the wireless room for a brief rest. Shortly before the change-over of the crew both on the bridge and in the crow's nest, Lightoller ordered Moody to take a message to the look-outs, instructing them 'to keep a sharp look out for ice, particularly small ice and growlers' and that the message be passed on to the look-outs due to come on duty at 10.00am. Not convinced that Moody had passed the message on correctly, Lightoller ordered him to undertake the duty again.

10.00pm – First Officer Murdoch took over the watch from Lightoller whilst Fred

Fleet and Reginald Lee took over from Jewel and Symons as look-outs; Symons passed on Lightoller's warning about icebergs to his replacements. Outside temperature had again dropped, this time to 32°F.

10.30pm – With his ship approaching a large icefield, Captain Lord on board the Californian decided to stop for the night and orders his sole wireless operator, Cyril Evans, to warn other ships about the proximity of ice. At about the same time Titanic passes the eastbound SS Rappahannock. More signals were exchanged between the two vessels in which the captain of the Rappahannock reported that his rudder had been damaged by ice and that the ship 'had just passed through heavy ice field and several icebergs.' The signal was acknowledged from the bridge of the Titanic 'Message received. Thank you. Good night.' As the Rappahannock was not fitted with a wireless, these messages were transmitted from the bridge; it was unfortunate that the Rappahannock was not fitted with a wireless as, apart from the mystery ship, she was probably the closest vessel to the Titanic when the iceberg was struck although her manoeuvrability would have been impaired by the damaged rudder.

11.00pm – Evans tried to pass a message to the Titanic about the presence of ice – 'We are stopped and surrounded by ice.' – but Jack Phillips, trying to clear a backlog of messages caused by the failure of the radio equipment earlier in the day, cut him off replying 'Shut up. I am busy, I am working Cape Race.'

11.30pm – Cyril Evans switched off his radio on board the Californian and retires to bed; this meant that any further wireless transmissions from the Titanic would be missed by the crew of the Californian.

11.39pm – Lookouts Frederick Fleet and Reginald Lee spot a large iceberg and the alarm bell was sounded three times by Fleet as he called the bridge and relayed the message 'Iceberg, right ahead'. Immediately, Murdoch, who had been on the starboard (open) wing of the bridge, rushed in, having seen the iceberg some 800 yards ahead himself, and ordered both 'Hard-a-starboard' and 'Stop: Full Speed Astern'. The Titanic had managed to turn 22.5° to port before the iceberg struck. (After the event, experiments were carried out with the Olympic that proved that at 21.5 knots, it would take 37 seconds to change course by 22.5° in a distance of 466 yards.) At the same time, Murdoch also pulled the lever that automatically closed the 15 watertight doors in the bulkheads.

11.40pm – The Titanic struck the iceberg. The ship was damaged for some 300 feet below the water line and some 15 feet above the keel. The intermittent gash extended through the forepeak tank, holds number one, two and three, and the forward boiler room (No six); in all it was later estimated that some 12 square feet in all had been opened up to the sea. The actual impact was variously described after the event but most remarked on how slight the bump felt. Captain Smith, having been woken by the collision, returned to the bridge and asked Murdoch 'What have we struck, Mr Murdoch? Murdoch replied that it was an iceberg and that it had been too close to take effective avoiding action. Smith then enquired about the status of the watertight doors and Murdoch confirmed that they had been closed. Apart from the automatic doors on the lower decks, there were also a number of watertight doors that could be closed manually. These non-automatic doors were hinged and secured by use of 12 clips. Again these doors were closed although, as elsewhere, these would have been of little practical purpose once the water started to rise above the actual level of the bulkheads.

12 midnight – Fleet and Lee are relieved as look-outs by Hogg and Evans; the new look-outs remain at their post in the crow's nest until about 12.30am although the telephone link between them and the bridge seems not to have functioned. The air temperature had fallen to 27°F (-2°C) and the sea temperature was 28°F.

12.05am – Captain Smith ordered the uncovering of the lifeboats; the floor of the squash court on F deck, some 32 feet above the keel was awash and water was entering boiler room No 5, the sixth watertight compartment from the stern.

12.10am – Captain Smith ordered the lifeboats to be swung out ready for use. Boxhall estimated the ship's position to be 41°46'N/50°14'W based around the accurate position taken at 7.30pm and his estimation of distance travelled since then.

12.15am – Captain Smith went to the wireless room and told Jack Phillips 'You had better get that assistance'. Phillips immediately sent out the first distress call – 'CQD'. ('CQD' – 'Come Quick, Danger– was the recognised distress signal; the more familiar signal today – 'SOS' – had only been introduced in 1907, following the International Conference on Wireless Communication at Sea held in Berlin the previous year, and was not yet in universal use. The decision made in 1906 was only ratified internationally in 1908 but British operators preferred to continue using the tradition 'CQD' signal.) Bride reported to the inquiry the conversation that he and

Phillips had had in the wireless room and that he had suggested 'Send SOS; it's the new call, and it may be your last chance to send it.' Phillips continued to use 'CQD' until 12.45am when he sent out his first 'SOS'). The first distress message was heard by the French steam La Provence and by the Canadian Pacific ship Mount Temple. The Mount Temple attempted to reply but the ship's wireless was not powerful enough. The position given in the first distress call was 41°44'N/50°24'W, which was incorrect.

12.15am – The orchestra, led by Wallace Hartley, started playing rag time numbers in the first class lounge before moving to the Boat Deck by the port-side entrance to the grand staircase. By this time the water had reached 40 feet above the keel at the forward end of Deck E.

12.18am – The Ypiranga picked up a distress signal; this time the location was given as 41°44'N/51°14'W. The ship receives the same message 10 times.

12.25am – Captain Smith ordered that women and children be loaded on to the prepared lifeboats. At about the same time he ordered the ship's pumps into action; the failure to take this basic action earlier remains one of the most surprising aspects of the sinking. The Carpathia receives a 'CQD' message from the Titanic: 'Come at once. We have struck a berg. It's a CQD, OM [Old Man] Position 41°46'N/50°24'W.' The message was also received by the land-based wireless station at Cape Race and passed on.

12.26am – A longer distress signal heard from Titanic: 'CQD. Here corrected position 41°46'N/50°14'W. Require immediate assistance. We have collision with iceberg. Sinking. Can hear nothing for noise of steam.' This was heard by the Ypiranga

NEXT PAGE
A telegraph sent to the Olympic with distress message.

and repeated 15 times. It was followed by a further message from the Titanic: 'I require assistance immediately. Struck by iceberg in 41°46'N/50°14'W.'

12.30am – The Frankfurt received a message from the Titanic: 'Tell your captain to come to our help. We are on ice.'

12.45am – Fourth Officer Joseph Boxhall launched the first white distress rocket; the exact number of distress rockets eventually fired is uncertain, with estimates ranging from eight to more than 20. Lawrence Beesley commented on the firing of the first rocket: 'Up it went, higher and higher, with a sea of faces upturned to watch it, and then an explosion that seemed to split the silent night in two.' At the same time the first lifeboat, No 7, was launched with only 28 people on board. These included the actress Dorothy Gibson, the French aviator Pierre Marechal, the Pennsylvanian banker James R McGough and William T Sloper. At the same time, Smith ordered Lightoller to fire the first distress rocket. Lightoller ordered all women and children to descend to A deck in order to gain entrance to the lifeboats from that level rather than the boat deck. Unfortunately, the windows on A deck were locked and, rather than lift the boats again to the boat deck, Lightoller ordered that the key be found. Amongst the passengers awaiting the location of the key at this location were a number of first class passengers, including Mrs Astor, Mrs Ryerson, Mrs Thayer and Mrs Widener. Phillips issued his first 'SOS' message to the Olympic, which was then some 500 nautical miles away.

12.50am – Titanic radioed Olympic (one of a number of messages monitored by Cottam on board the Carpathia): 'I require immediate assistance.'

12.55am – Lifeboat No 5 with 39 passengers and crew on board was launched; as it descended two male passengers, Dr H W Frauenthal and his brother, leapt on board, joining the doctor's wife who was already on board. One of the other passengers, Mrs Annie May Stengel, was slightly injured as she was hit by the jumping men.

1.00am – Lifeboat No 3 was launched with 25 women and children and, at the last minute, 10 male passengers were also allowed to join as there were no other women and children immediately present. A total of 15 members of crew were also on board No 3 as it was lowered, making a total of 50 in all. Also launched at about this time was port side lifeboat No 6; this was occupied by 25 women and two crew members – Fleet and Hitchens – and Mrs James Joseph 'Molly' Brown, one of the 25 women, demanded that an extra crewman be allocated. There was no crewman immediately available and so Lightoller permitted Major Arthur Godfrey Peuchen, an experienced yachtsman as well as a passenger, to board. With Hitchens refusing to row, the indomitable Mrs Brown took up an oar and was soon followed by a number of the other women. Whilst at sea, lifeboat No 6 picked up another crew member, a stoker.

1.02am – The Titanic sent a message to the Asian requesting assistance.

1.10am – Lifeboat No 1 was launched. On board were 12 people, including Sir Cosmo and Lady Duff-Gordon, on a lifeboat designed for a maximum of 40. Lifeboats Nos 1 and 2 were smaller – at 25 feet in length – than the other lifeboats fitted (which were all 30 feet in length) and were deemed emergency boats. The boat was nominally under the control of one of the look-outs, George Symons.

1.10am – Lifeboat No 8 was launched with 24 passengers and four members of crew on board. This was the lifeboat approached by Mr and Mrs Straus. A further message was sent from the Titanic to the Olympic: 'We are in collision with berg. Sinking, head down, come as soon as possible. Get your boats ready.'

1.20am – Lifeboat No 9 was launched with 56 on board – eight crew members, 42 women and children, and six male passengers. Also launched at 1.20am was lifeboat No 10 with 55 on board, including five members of crew to handle the boat once it hit the water.

1.25am – Lifeboat No 11 was launched – with about 70 on board – and the last distress rocket fired. This was followed by lifeboat No 12 with 43 passengers and crew on board. Next to be released was lifeboat No 14 with up to 64 on board; as this was lowered, the mechanism seized up with the boat some five feet above the water. Lowe reacted by pulling the lever of Murray's Patented Release Gear, which released both ends of the lifeboat simultaneously. The boat fell into the water with some force, causing a leak to spring. Until those on board were rescued by the Carpathia the boat had to be baled out manually by hand with the use of hats. A third message from the Titanic to the Olympic was picked up by the Carpathia: 'We are putting the women off in small boats.'

1.35am – Lifeboat No 16 was lowered with 56 passengers and crew on board; whilst the lifeboat was being lowered, one of the stewardesses on board, Mrs Leather, heard the band still playing under Wallace Hartley. At the same time lifeboat No 13 was lowered from the starboard side. This provided accommodation for nine crewmen, three stewardesses, three first class passengers

Form No. **4.—100**— 17.8.10.

Thé Marconi Inter

WATERGATE HO

No. "O L Y M P I C"

Handed in at ——— TITANIC

This message has been transmitted subject to which have been agreed to by the Sender. If the Receiver, on paying the necessary charges, may Office to Office over the Company's system, and charges for such repetition will be refunded. respecting this Telegram.

To OLYMPIC

Eleven pm NEW YORK

ANSWERED HIS CALLS

TITANIC REPLIES AN

"WE HAVE STRUCK AN

OUR DISTANCE FROM

Deld. Date 14 APR 1912

al Marine Communication Co., Ltd.,

RK BUILDINGS, ADELPHI, LONDON, W.C.

OFFICE. 14 Apr 19 12

CHARGES TO PAY.

Total			

printed on the back hereof,
is message be doubted, the
d whenever possible, from
rror be shown to exist, all
st accompany any enquiry

TITANIC SENDING OUT SIGNALS OF DISTRESS

S ME HIS POSITION 41.46 N 50 14 W AND SAYS

ERG".

C 505 MILES.

and 49 second and third class women and children as well as two others, a total of 66. As the boat was being lowered, one of the crewmen noticed Lawrence Beesley and asked if there were any women and children visible. When Beesley indicated that he couldn't see any, the crewmen instructed Beesley to leap aboard, taking the number on board lifeboat No 13 to 67. Simultaneously, lifeboat No 15 was lowered; for a time it looked as though it would descend directly on top of No 13, but shouts from those in No 13 were heard and the lowering of No 15 was delayed fractionally. A total of 68 or 70 escaped on board No 15. A fourth message was sent from the Titanic: 'Engine room getting flooded.'

1.40am – Collapsible lifeboat C, with 39 people on board was lowered; this was the lifeboat on which J Bruce Ismay made his escape. The boat was originally designed to accommodate 47 and, according to Ismay, he stepped aboard as it was being lowered, in the company of another first class passenger (Mr Carter), as he became aware that there was still space on it. Cape Race sent a message to the Virginian: 'Please tell your Captain this: The Olympic is making all speed for Titanic, but his [ie the Olympic's] position is 40°32'N/61°18'W. You are much closer to Titanic. The Titanic is already putting women off in the boats, and he says the weather there is "calm and clear". The Olympic is the only ship we have heard say, "going to the assistance of the Titanic." The others must be a long way from the Titanic.' The last distress rocket was fired from the Titanic.

1.45am – Lifeboat No 2, with Fourth Officer Boxhall in charge, was lowered. As with No 1, this had a smaller capacity – 40 – than the other 14 lifeboats but only 25 were on board when it was launched. A fifth and

final message was picked up by the Carpathia: 'Engine room full up to the boilers…' The wireless room log on board the Carpathia recorded that at '12.20am [2.10am Titanic time] Signals were broken'.

1.47am – The Caronia heard a message from the Titanic, but the signal was weak and couldn't be read.

1.48am – The Asian heard an 'SOS' from the Titanic but couldn't get a response to its reply.

1.50am – The Caronia heard transmissions between the Frankfurt and the Titanic; this was the last message that the Caronia heard transmitted from the latter.

1.55am – Lifeboat No 4 was launched; this was the last conventional lifeboat and it departed with 40 people on board; 25 seats remained unoccupied. Amongst those on board was 13-year-old Jack Myerson; initially Lightoller tried to prevent him boarding but was outvoted by those on board. This was the boat that the Astors tried to board and was the last time that John Jacob Astor was seen alive. One of the crewmen on board, greaser Thomas Grainger, heard that the band was still playing as the lifeboat was lowered. Cape Race sent a message to the Virginian: 'We have not heard Titanic for about half an hour. His power may be gone.' (The signals from the Titanic would grow weaker as power from the generators declined. As the generators were powered by the boilers, as the water level increased so the efficiency of the generators declined. The wireless equipment was fitted with emergency batteries and so could continue to operate once the main generators failed provided that the operators had had the opportunity to switchover to them.)

2.00am – The rising water reached the forward boat deck. The Virginian heard a faint signal from the Titanic but nothing further.

2.05am – The water had now reached the bottom of the bridge rail and the ship's propellers were rising out of the water. Collapsible lifeboat D was lowered with 37 women and children along with three crew members aboard. As it was lowered, three men – Hugh Woolner, H B Steffanson and Frederick Hoyt – jumped on board. Hoyt missed and had to be rescued from the water. At about the same time Captain Smith relieved Bride and Phillips from their duty in the wireless room saying 'Men you have done your full duty, you can do no more. Abandon your cabin'.

2.10am – Sea water swept over the forward end of the boat deck, freeing collapsible lifeboat B and washing it overboard. Collapsible lifeboat A was also launched – under circumstances that are uncertain – and a number of survivors clambered aboard. Unfortunately, the collapsible sides failed with the result that the boat was semi-flooded resulting in it ultimately providing sanctuary for no more than 14 survivors by the time they were rescued by the Carpathia.

2.17am – The alleged final sighting of Captain Smith as he entered the bridge for the last time.

2.18am – The ship's electrical system finally failed. Of the Titanic's 34 engineering officers who had struggled to keep power going to the very end, not one deserted their post and not one was to survive. According to Lord Beresford 'Had it not been for their steadfast dedication to duty, many more lives would have been lost'.

2.20am – The Titanic finally sank, breaking its back between the third and fourth funnels. The stern section remains afloat a few moments longer than the bow section.

2.45am – The Second Officer on the Carpathia, James Bisset, spotted the first iceberg. Captain Rostron later commented 'It lay two points on the port bow and it was one whose presence was betrayed by the star beam. More and more we were all keyed up. Icebergs loomed up and fell astern; we never slackened, though sometimes we altered course suddenly to avoid them. It was an anxious time with the Titanic's fateful experience very close in our minds. There were 700 souls on the Carpathia; these lives, as well as all the survivors of the Titanic itself depended on a sudden turn of the wheel.'

3.30am – The rockets from the RMS Carpathia under Captain Arthur Henry Rostron first spotted by the survivors in the lifeboats.

4.00am – Having safely negotiated the icefield to the point where the Titanic was believed to have sunk, Captain Rostron ordered the engines of the Carpathia to be stopped whilst the crew scanned the sea for evidence of wreckage and survivors. Nothing was immediately visible. Suddenly, a crew member spotted a green light close to the water; it was a flare from lifeboat No 2 under the command of Joseph Boxhall.

4.10am – Following some minor manoeuvring, the RMS Carpathia reached the site and started to pick up survivors from the lifeboats. The first person to be taken on board the Carpathia was first class passenger Elizabeth Allen from lifeboat No 2; she confirmed that the Titanic had indeed sunk. Apart from the passengers, the Carpathia also takes on board most of the Titanic's lifeboats (with the exception of the collapsible boats and lifeboat No 14).

4.10am – Lifeboat No 7 came alongside the Carpathia and its passengers taken aboard.

4.30am – Captain Lord on the Californian was awakened by George V Stewart, the officer of the watch.

4.45am – Lifeboat No 13, the eighth or ninth to come alongside the Carpathia, arrived at the Cunard ship; the passengers are taken aboard.

5.15am – As the day dawns, Captain Lord ordered the engines of the Californian started. Spotting a vessel that he believed to be in distress, he ordered that Evans, the ship's wireless operator be roused. Having switched on his wireless, Evans issues a 'CQ' message – 'All stations, someone answer'. He received an immediate reply from the German-owned Frankfurt telling him that the Titanic had sunk during the night at 41°46'N/50°14'W – a position that Lord estimated to be some 19.5 miles from the Californian's current position. He orders the ship southwards to make for the Titanic's last known position at top speed (13.5 knots).

6.00am – Lifeboat No 3 came alongside the Carpathia and its passengers were taken aboard.

6.15am – The passengers from collapsible lifeboat C were picked up by the Carpathia.

6.30am – Having carefully made progress through the icefield, the Californian reached open water. About the same time, the survivors on board the upturned collapsible B were picked up by lifeboat No 12, meaning that this boat was now offering accommodation for some 70 passengers and crew all now under the command of Lightoller.

7.00am – Lifeboat 14, under the command of Fifth Officer Lowe, towing

collapsible lifeboat D went alongside the Carpathia.

7.30am – The Californian encounters the Almerian – a vessel not equipped with wireless – at the point recorded as being the Titanic's last known position. However, there was no evidence of wreckage or survivors. However, the Carpathia was spotted to the southeast and the Californian headed towards her.

8.00am – Lifeboat No 6, under the command of Quartermaster Robert Hitchens,

with Frederick Fleet and Arthur Peuchen, came alongside the Carpathia.

8.30am – The final lifeboat to be picked up – the overloaded lifeboat No 12 under the command of Second Officer Herbert Lightoller – was pulled alongside the Carpathia. Shortly afterwards, the Californian arrives alongside – the two ships are operating at 41°33'N/50°01'W.

8.50am – With the arrival of the Californian to continue the search for survivors, the Carpathia departed the site of the sinking to make for New York with the survivors on board.

10.30am – Having searched the area of the sinking, the Californian resumes its trip to Boston. At 10.25am the following day, the Californian sends a wireless message to the Carpathia: 'Searched vicinity of disaster until noon yesterday, saw very little wreckage, no bodies, no sign of missing boat, regards Lord.'

Chapter Thirteen

Aftermath

RIGHT
A newspaper shows the brief career of the Titanic.

Following the sinking, and the recovery of the survivors, a total of 705 were found to have survived the sinking. Unfortunately, the completely accurate figure is unknown, but 705 is generally regarded as the norm. The number of fatalities is also uncertain, but the total is generally recognised to be between 1,502 and 1,523, making it the worst sea disaster to have occurred up to that point in history.

Having departed from the scene of the sinking later on the morning of 15 April, the Carpathia docked at Pier 54 during the evening of 18 April at about 9.35pm. Prior to docking, the ship had deposited the Titanic's lifeboats at Pier 59, as they were the property of White Star Line. Vast crowds witnessed the survivors disembarking from the Carpathia. In order to assist, the US Immigration Service allowed all the passengers, irrespective of class, immediate access to land; normally, those seeking immigration into the country would have been transferred to Ellis Island for processing, but on this occasions this examination was waived. The last people to be transferred from the Carpathia were the surviving members of the crew. They were transferred to the US Immigration Service's tender, the George Starr, and transferred to accommodation on board the Red Star Line Lapland. Red Star Line was another shipping line controlled by International Mercantile Marine.

In order to recover the bodies, White Star Line chartered the cable ship CS Mackay-Bennett from Halifax, Nova Scotia, and this ship along with three others – the Minia (another cable ship), Montmagny (a lighthouse supply ship belonging to Canadian Ministry of Marine and Fisheries) and Algerine (a sealing vessel) – recovered 328 bodies; a further five were recovered by passing steamships. Of the 333 recovered, 124 were buried at sea with the remainder being returned to Halifax, where the local coroner exercised jurisdiction.

A number of the bodies recovered – 59 – were reclaimed by members of their families and transported either to the USA or back to Britain for burial. The majority – 150 – were, however, buried in any one of the three cemeteries in Halifax. Of the bodies recovered, 128 remained unidentified despite the best efforts of the crews of the recovery ships in trying to ensure that all evidence of identity was secured. The burials of those brought back to Halifax commenced on 3 May 1912. Of the 128 unidentified, one was to affect the crew of the Mackay-Bennett profoundly; this was the body of a two-year-old boy. When it came to the child's burial, Captain Lardner of the Mackay-Bennett and his crew paid for the service and for a gravestone. More recent research has suggested that the child was one of a Scandinavian migrant family and that, if the

DEPARTURE   —THE LEVIATHAN (AND HER COMMANDER, CAPTAIN SMITH) LEAVING SOUTHAMPTON—   APRIL 10

DOOM   —THE FATE OF THE TITANIC, ILLUSTRATED BY ICEBERGS FLOATING IN THE ATLANTIC—   APRIL 14, 10.25 P.M.

DAILY GRAPHIC

ACCIDENT **£1,000** INSURANCE

TUESDAY, APRIL 16, 1912.

TITANIC SUNK: APPALLING LOSS of LIFE

PRESS   —SCENES AT THE WHITE STAR OFFICES IN COCKSPUR STREET AND THE CITY—   APRIL

tentative identification is correct, he is buried close to the grave of his mother.

With such a loss of life, it was inevitable that inquiries would be held into the causes of the accident and the lessons that could be learnt from it. The American Inquiry formally opened on 19 April and was chaired by Senator William Alden Smith although the initial work had been undertaken on the Carpathia when it docked on the 18th and when Smith first interviewed J Bruce Ismay.

William Alden Smith (12 May 1859 to 11 October 1932), a Republican Senator from Michigan, headed a six-man commission, formed of three Democrats and three

Republicans, that sat for 17 days between 19
April and 25 May. He was a lawyer, builder
and railway operator but was characterised in
the US press as being something of a fool. This
may be that he was from the mid-west rather
than from the more sophisticated east coast.
He was, however, antipathetic to J P Morgan's
business interests and was also conscious
that under the terms of the 1898 Harter Act
shipping lines could be sued in the event of
an accident if negligence could be proved. He

New York, Smith interviewed a total of 82
witnesses, 53 of whom were British and the
rest US citizens. Of these, two were officers
from International Mercantile Marine, four
were the surviving officers from the Titanic
itself, 34 were members of the ship's crew
and 21 were passengers (with representatives
from all three classes). There were a total of
1,145 pages of testimony and when Alden
reported, his report extended to some 19
pages with a further 44 pages of evidence.
The cost of the US enquiry was some $6,600.

was, however, to prove highly objective in his
work and in his ultimate report.

During the course of his inquiry, which
was held in the Waldorf-Astoria Hotel in

Alden came up with two main
recommendations, both of which were
swiftly converted into legislation. The first
concerned lifeboats and the necessity both
of providing sufficient for all passengers

and crew and that sufficient training in their use needed to be given. The second recommendation related to the use of radios and the need to ensure that all ships kept them manned 24 hours a day with adequate power supply and action to prevent interference.

At about 10am on 20 April, the Lapland, on which the surviving members of the Titanic's crew had been housed since their arrival in New York, set sail back to Britain. However, before she set sail, 29 subpoenas were served to ensure that relevant members of the ship's crew remained in New York to assist the US inquiry. The surviving four officers and 34 other ratings remained in New York for this purpose. It has been suggested that White Star Line was keen to ensure that its staff were not able to present evidence to the inquiry but, given the fact that sailors ceased to be paid from the moment their ship sank and a human desire to return the survivors to their loved ones as soon as possible, the company was probably acting in the interests of the survivors rather than for any ulterior motive.

The Lapland reached Plymouth at around 7.00am on 29 April and dropped anchor in Cowsand Bay at around 7.30am. Three tenders came out to the ship: two were to transport the passengers whilst the third – the Sir Richard Grenville – was to bring the Titanic's crew ashore. Despite the presence of a vast crowd of family members, press and others, the survivors were not immediately allowed to depart as the representatives of the Board of Trade present were determined to try and interview the survivors. Initially, the crew were reluctant to answer questions but, with the arrival of their union representatives, this process could start and later that day and

on the 30th the British survivors were finally allowed to make their way home.

A week later, on 6 May, the Celtic docked at Liverpool; on board was a further batch of crew members, including Fleet, Lee and Robert Hitchens. The body of Wallace Hartley arrived back in Liverpool on board the Arabic on 12 May and on 18 May Harold Bride arrived back at Liverpool on board the Baltic. This was followed on the 21st by the arrival of the Adriatic to Liverpool with

Ismay on board in the company of Lightoller, Lowe and Pitman.

The British Inquiry, chaired by the Wreck Commissioner of the Board of Trade, John Charles Bigham (Lord Mersey), was held between 2 May and 3 July. The building selected for the inquiry was the Drill Hall of the London Scottish Regiment, which was located close to Buckingham Palace. Whilst this was a large building, capable of holding several hundred people (as interest from the press and public was expected to be great), the acoustics left much to be desired. The inquiry set itself to answer 26 questions covering the construction of state of the ship as she sailed from Southampton, the journey across the Atlantic and the warnings received, the damage received by the ship and the actual sinking, and how those survived were rescued. During the course of the inquiry a further question – on the role of Captain Lord and the Californian – also entered.

In order to aid the deliberations of Lord Mersey and his assessors, a 20-foot model of the Titanic – built like the original by Harland & Wolff – was displayed behind the witness box and also visible were a large plan of the north Atlantic and a 40-foot long side plan of the ship, the latter designed to illustrate the complexity of the ship in terms of possible evacuation.

The Board of Trade was represented at the inquiry by the Attorney General, Sir Rufus Daniel Isaacs KC, who was assisted by the Solicitor General, Sir John Simon. It was the latter who raised the initial list of questions that the inquiry was designed to try and answer. White Star Line was represented by the Right Honourable Sir

Robert Finlay KC MP whilst the National Sailors' & Firemen's Union was represented,

on the instructions of Captain Smith's widow, by Thomas Scanlan MP. A number of other parties were, however, denied representation; these included Captain Lord and the Californian, whose representative, C Robertson Dunlop, was allowed only to act as an observer and could not have any direct role in the inquiry.

Following opening submissions, the inquiry team travelled to Southampton on 6 May 1912 in order to see for themselves the Olympic, which had been made available for the inspection. Back at the Drill Hall, the inquiry examined a wide range of those involved in the disaster itself, both crew and survivors, as well as noted experts such as the famous Arctic explorer Sir Ernest Shackleton. Captain Lord himself gave evidence on the seventh day of the inquiry. Apart from him, other members of the crew of the Californian were also interviewed as were Captain Rostron and the crew of the Carpathia. By 21 June, when the taking of testimony ceased, a total of 25,622 questions had been asked and answered. Following a further eight days of summations and closing arguments, the inquiry adjourned to allow Lord Mersey to complete his report. He presented his conclusions at the end of July 1912. Amongst his many comments were three and a half pages criticising Captain Lord and the failure of the Californian to make greater efforts to reach the stricken ship.

The British Inquiry concluded that 'the loss of the said ship was due to collision with an iceberg brought on by the excessive speed at which the ship was being navigated'. It had been claimed, although the evidence for this was limited and disputed by many, that J Bruce Ismay had encouraged Captain Smith to push the Titanic to the maximum and

clearly the British Inquiry was of the opinion that, given the prevailing conditions, the captain should have been more cautious.

Following both inquiries, a number of changes were made to maritime practice, ship design and operation, all designed to ensure that a similar tragedy could not recur in future. On 12 November 1913 the first International Convention for the Safety of Life at Sea was convened in London. On 30 January 1914 a treaty was signed that led to the creation and funding of the International Ice Patrol. This, part of the United States Coast Guard, continues in operation to the present day and is tasked with monitoring and reporting all icebergs identified in the North Atlantic that might pose a threat to

transatlantic shipping. Ship designs were modified to incorporate deeper bulkheads and the use of double-hull technology. Reflecting the conclusions of the British Inquiry, the Board of Trade in London introduced regulations instructing captains to reduce speed if there was any likelihood of meeting icebergs.

Of all the consequences of the sinking of the Titanic, the most significant was perhaps critical. The historic belief that sufficient lifeboats were not required as those available would be adequate to ferry passengers and crew from the stricken vessel to one of the many other vessels that would have responded to the distress signals had proved fallacious.

Following the two inquiries, there was the question of litigation and compensation. Under the terms of the Merchant Ships Act, White Star Line was liable for the freight lost, £123,711, but there were also claims lodged in US courts for personal losses of lives and goods; total claims lodged in the USA amounted to $16,804,112 although the company took action to limit its liabilities under American law. As the Titanic was sailing to New York and as the company's main US office was based in the city, it was the United States District Court, Southern District of New York under Judge Charles M Hough that heard the case. In an earlier judgement, Hough's fellow New York judge, George C Holt, had ruled that British law held jurisdiction over the limits to the total claim. The claims for loss of property extended from William Carter's Renault 35hp car (valued at $5,000) to a copy of the magazine *Science & Health* for which Annie May Stengel claimed $5.00. Legal action in both the USA and UK dragged on until, in late 1915, lawyers for both parties reached the outline of a settlement; this was concluded on 28 July 1916, when Judge Julius M Mayer (who had succeeded Judge Hough in June 1915) signed a decree terminating all law suits. A total of $663,000 was distributed, following this agreement, amongst the individual claimants.

Chapter Fourteen

The Rescue & Recovery Ships

There are a number of other ships that will always be inextricably linked to the sinking of the Titanic. Of these, the most important are perhaps the SS Californian and the RMS Carpathia.

Owned by the Leyland Line – and thus ultimately controlled by J P Morgan's International Mercantile Marine like the White Star Line – the Californian was a steam ship built by the Caledon Shipbuilding & Engineering Co of Dundee. Launched on 26 November 1901, the ship began its maiden voyage from Dundee to New Orleans, following sea trials, on 31 January 1902. It first reached New Orleans on 3 March 1902. The Californian was 447 feet long and 53 feet at its beam, weighing 6,223 tons. With a crew of 55 the ship was capable of carrying a maximum of 47 passengers at an average speed of 12 knots. Stanley Lord had been appointed captain of the Californian in 1911 and, on 5 April 1912, was in command as the ship left London en route to Boston. The ship was making its transatlantic crossing on this occasion without any passengers on board. During the evening of 14 April, the Californian encountered icebergs and Lord decided to stop engines and await daylight before attempting to

navigate through the ice. There has been some debate about what actually happened on board the Californian during the night of 14/15 April 1912, particularly as a result of contradictory evidence given by the ship's crew to the British inquiry, but the ship did finally reach the sight of the sinking at around 8.30am on the morning of the 15th. Following the departure of the Carpathia the Californian continued to search for survivors, before heading westwards to New York, where she arrived on 19 April 1912. Three members of the crew – Lord, Evans and Ernest Gil – gave evidence to the US inquiry before the ship and crew headed back to the UK. After the sinking of the Titanic, the Californian remained in service with Leyland Line until she was requisitioned by the British government in World War 1. She was to be sunk by a German submarine on 9 November 1915 some 61 miles southwest of Cape Matapan in Greece.

If the role of the SS Californian was open to criticism, that of the RMS Carpathia under Captain Arthur Rostron was not. Built by Swan Hunter & Wigham Richardson on the Tyne at Newcastle, the Carpathia was owned by Cunard Line. The ship had been launched on 6 August 1902 and commenced

BELOW
The bronze
medallion (red
ribbon), presented to
crewmen and officers
of the Carpathia.

her sea trials on 22 April the following year
before commencing her maiden voyage
from Liverpool to Boston on 5 May 1903.
The ship weighed 8,600 tons and was 541
feet in length and with a beam of 64.5 feet.
Rostron had been appointed captain of the
Californian in January 1912 and, on 11
April 1912, the ship had set off from New
York Pier 54 for a transatlantic crossing to
Fiume, via Gibraltar, Genoa, Naples and
Trieste. On board were 128 first, 50 second
and 565 third class passengers. Initially First
Officer Horace Dean, who was on the
bridge, doubted the veracity of the distress
calls received by the ship's wireless operator,

Harold Cottam, but, when roused, Rostron
took immediate action and set a course to
the Titanic's last known position, some
58 miles away. In an exemplary display of
seamanship, Rostron made preparations for
the receipt of potential survivors. Amongst
the actions that he took were to order all
crew to duty; the preparation of all lifeboats;
the running of electric lights along the ship's
hull; the setting up of block and tackle at
each gangway door; the setting up of bags
on hoists in order to facilitate the lifting of
children; the dropping of pilot ladders and
side ladders as well as the hanging of cargo
nets over the side in order to allow survivors

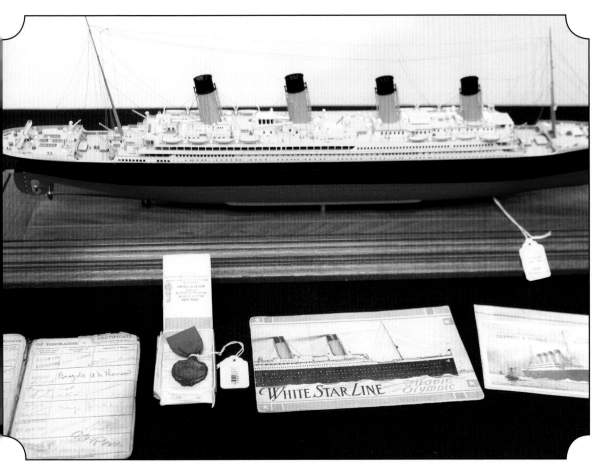

Chapter Fourteen

to clamber up; the preparation of steam hoists in order to allow for the lifting of any cargo and mail; the setting up of first aid posts in the ship's dining rooms and the gathering up of all available medication on board; the allocation of crew to take all names as they came aboard; the conversion of the ship's public rooms into dormitories in order to accommodate survivors and, all available bedding was gathered together. Without these preparations, the actual rescue of the survivors would have proved much more problematic.

The Carpathia was originally designed for a maximum of only 14 knots but, by maximising the boiler room crew and by switching off the steam heating to the passengers' cabins, he was able to maintain pressure and thus obtain a remarkable 17 knots from the engine. Not only was this a remarkable achievement in its own right, but he was also sailing at more than

full speed into an area in which ice was a constant threat – indeed the Carpathia passed six icebergs and had to take avoiding action to miss another six all without reducing speed. Again demonstrating his consummate seamanship, Rostron had taken the precaution of doubling the look-outs in both the bow and crow's nest as well as stationing additional look-outs on either side of the bridge. Rather than the five hours that

the sailing should have taken, the Carpathia arrived at the site of the sinking some four hours after first being alerted. Between 4am and 8.30am the ship rescued more than 700 survivors from the sea before being relieved by the Californian and heading back to New York. The Carpathia reached New York on 18 April. The RMS Carpathia remained in service with Cunard but, like the Californian, was to be torpedoed by a German submarine (U-55) whilst on convoy duty on 17 July 1918 to the east of Ireland. A total of 157 passengers and crew were rescued.

The Mount Temple was built by Armstrong, Whitworth & Co of Newcastle upon Tyne and launched in June 1901. Owned by Elder, Dempster & Co, the Mount Temple started her maiden voyage between the River Tyne and New Orleans on 19 September 1901. Following two trips to South Africa carrying troops to the Boer War, the ship was sold to Canadian Pacific, along with 14 other vessels and Elder Dempster's Canadian route, in 1903. After serving on the Liverpool-Montreal route, she was transferred to the service linking London with St John, New Brunswick, and it was whilst on this service that she was in the vicinity of the Titanic when the White Star liner sank. Following the outbreak of war in August 1914, the Mount Temple was briefly used as a troop ship from September 1914 before returning to commercial service in 1915. On 6 December 1916 she was captured by the German raider Mowe some 600 miles west of Fastnet. Once the surviving passengers and crew were removed, the ship was sunk by the Germans.

The CS Mackay-Bennett was a London-registered cable repair ship owned by the Commercial Cable Company and was normally based in Halifax, Nova Scotia. Built in 1884, she was 259.3 feet long and had a beam of 40.1 feet. Her registered tonnage was 1,631 tons. She was the first of four vessels chartered by White Star Line to search for bodies. Under the command of Captain Frederick Harold Larnder, and with an all-volunteer crew (that received double pay for the dreadful work ahead) the Mackay-Bennett cost White Star Line US $550 per day. She set sail from Halifax at 12.28pm on Wednesday 17 April and, after her arrival at the site of the sinking, the number of bodies visible indicated that a further vessel would be required and White Star then chartered the Minia. The Mackay-Bennett first reached the wreck site at 8.00pm on the evening of 20 April and started to recover the bodies on the following day. The Mackay-Bennett recovered a total of 306 bodies, with 116 being buried at sea – the first funeral service was held on 21 April when 24 bodies were buried at sea – with the remainder being embalmed for return to Halifax. Of those buried at sea, only 56 could be identified. On 26 April, the Mackay-Bennett met up with the Minia and then departed back to Halifax, where she berthed at 9.30am on 30 April 1912 in the city's naval dockyard. The Mackay-Bennett sailed with both a cleric and team of undertakers on board; the former for handling any religious services the latter to embalm the bodies for the trip to Canada. The subsequent search vessels also were thus provided with the exception of the Algerine, which seems to have sailed without a minister on board.

The CS Minia was owned by Western Union – previously the Anglo-American Telegraph Co – and was under the command of Captain William George Squares deCarteret. Built in 1860, the Minia was 328.5 feet in length with a beam of 35.8 feet and a registered tonnage of 2,061 tons. She departed from Halifax on 22 April and reached the wreck site on the 26th. Having briefly met up with the Mackay-Bennett the Minia continued the search after the earlier ship had departed back to Halifax. However, poor weather meant that the ship's search was hampered and a total of only 17 bodies were

recovered; of these two unidentified firemen were buried at sea with the remainder returned, with the ship, to Halifax on 6 May.

The third ship to be chartered by White Star Line was the lighthouse supply vessel the Montmagny, which was operated by the Canadian Department of Marine and Fisheries and was under the command of Captain Peter Crerar Johnson – international waters – and Capitaine François-Xavier Pouliot – domestic waters. The ship had been built in 1909 and was 212.6 feet in length with a beam of 34.8 feet. Her registered tonnage was 1,269 tons. The ship sailed from Sorel, Quebec, where she had been built, to Halifax, departing from Halifax after supplies had been transferred from the Minia on 6 May. The weather again was difficult and only four additional bodies were recovered; one of these was buried at sea with the other three being landed at Louisbourg, Nova Scotia, on 13 May. The Montmagny returned to the search area but found no more bodies, departing the area on 19 May after the arrival of the final search vessel, the Algerine. She arrived back at Halifax on 23 May.

The fourth and final search vessels was the steamer Algerine; this ship, ironically, had been originally built by Harland & Wolff in 1880 before being rebuilt in 1910 and by 1912 was owned by Bowring Brothers of St Johns, Newfoundland. She was 172.1 feet in length and with a beam of 29.5 feet. Her registered tonnage was 505 tons and she was under the command of Captain John Jackman. The ship departed St Johns on 16 May 1912 and met up with the Montmagny on the 19th before the latter's return to Halifax. The Algerine was at sea for three weeks but was able to recover only one body – that of saloon steward James McGrady, whose remains were returned to Halifax on 6 June.

Last Sunday's Count of Want Ads
Post-Dispatch.... 7149
All 6011
Post-Dispatch Gain 384 | VOL. 64. NO. 240.

ST. L

1302 LIVES LOST

Carpathia Steaming t

NEW YORK, April 16.—Wireless from Capt. Roston of Ca sidered New York best. Large number icebergs and twenty mil

MONTREAL, April 16.—The Allan Line issues the follow the disaster too late to be of service and is proceeding to Liverpoo

HALIFAX, N. S., April 16.—The Allan Liner Parisian re

CAPE RACE, April 16.—Olympic reports by wireless "C n, 50:14w. ALL HER BOATS ACCOUNTED FOR, containing position of disaster.

Giant Steamer Titanic as it would appear alongside the Eads Br

7 ST. LOUISANS ARE REPORTED SAFE ON BOARD CARPATHIA

Mrs. Robert, Misses Madill and Allen, Hays and Wife Rescued and

POST-DISPATCH

in St. Louis With the Associated Press News Service.

TUESDAY EVENING, APRIL 16, 1912—28 PAGES. PRICE ONE CENT

HOME EDITION

N "TITANIC" SANK; 868 SAVED

York With Survivors; None on Other Ships

line here, reads:"Proceeding to New York with about 800. Consulted with Mr. Ismay. So much ice about. con-
rgs amongst."

We are in receipt of a Marconi via Cape Race, from Capt. Gambell of the Virginian, that he arrived on the scene of

da Sable Island, that she has no passengers from the Titanic on board.

Titanic position at daybreak FOUND BOATS AND WRECKAGE ONLY. Titanic sank about 2:20 a. m. in 41:16
ved, crew and passengers included. Nearly all saved women and children. Californian remained searching exact

phed off Newfoundland and St. Louis woman passenger rescued.

2-THIRDS WOMEN IN PARTIAL LIST OF THOSE RESCUED

Astor, Butt, Guggenheim and Many Other Famous Men Who Were on Board Not Mentioned Among Survivors---Money Loss Is $20,000,000.

ABOUT 2200 PERSONS WERE ABOARD TITANIC.

Passengers of all classes...1310
Crew 860
Women and children in first cabin 143
Women and children in second cabin 87

White Star line officials say that a small number of passengers may have been taken on after the booking list was made up, and that the crew may be a little larger or smaller than stated.

Lifeboats for Only One-Third on Board

NEW YORK, April 16.
THE Bureau of Inspection of

By Associated Press.

ST. JOHNS, Newfoundland, April 16. All hope that any of the passengers or any members of the crew of the Titanic other than those on the Carpathia are alive was abandoned here this afternoon. All of the steamers which have been cruising in the vicinity of the disaster have continued on their voyages.

HALIFAX, N. S., April 16. The liner Parisian has reported by wireless that she steamed through much heavy field ice looking for passengers from the ill-fated Titanic. No life rafts or bodies

Chapter Fifteen

Discovery

RIGHT
A section of th
Titanic's hul

BELOW
Bob Ballar
(pointing) wit
his crew

Almost from the moment that the Titanic sank there had been efforts to try and track the ship down although some of the proposals to try and salvage the vessel were perhaps farfetched. Early searches for the wreck were hampered by the fact that the last position reported by the ship – 41°46'N/50°14'W – was some 13 nautical miles (24kms) from the actual location (41°43'55"N/49°56'45"W) that the ship was ultimately discovered at.

It was not until 1 September 1985 that a joint US-French survey, led by Dr Robert Ballard of the Woods Hole Oceanographic Institution, Jean-Louis Michel of IFREMER and Dr Nicholas S E Cappon on board the research vessel Knorr, finally made the breakthrough. Using a remotely-controlled camera on board an unmanned submersible, Argo, the wreck was discovered at a depth of 12,000 feet to the southeast of Newfoundland. The discovery represented the culmination of almost two months of investigation.

The 1985 expedition, funded in part by National Geographic and by French taxpayers, was jointly organised by the Institut Français de Recherches pour l'Exploitation des Mers and the US Woods

Chapter Fifteen

Hole Oceanographic Institution. The French vessel Le Surôit sailed on 1 July 1985 for the wreck site, reaching the area on 9 July. For 10 days, using 3,000 feet wide sonar scans, the ship criss-crossed the north Atlantic searching for the wreck. Finding nothing, the ship sailed to the French territory of St Pierre et Miquelon, located just to the south of Newfoundland, for refuelling on 19 July. Whilst at St Pierre et Miquelon, the French crew was joined by Robert Ballard and other members of the Woods Hole team prior to sailing once more to the wreck site.

A further search of the area of the supposed wreck resumed on 26 July but, with 80% of the area surveyed by early August, time was running out on the first phase of the search as Le Surôit was required for other duties elsewhere. With the French ship withdrawn from the search, Dr Ballard and other scientists flew to the Azores where they joined the Woods Hole's own survey vessel, Knorr. Loaded on board the ship were two pieces of vital equipment – the submersibles Argo and Angus – that would prove essential in diving down to the depth of two and a half miles where the wreck was ultimately located. The Argo project had been part funded, to the tune of $2.8 million, by the United States Navy's Office of Naval Research. The Knorr sailed from Ponte Delgada on the Azores on 17 August but, before heading for the site of the Titanic, the crew diverted initially to survey the wreck of the USS Scorpion, a nuclear submarine that had been lost with all hands in 1968. The Knorr reached the search area on 22 August 1985 and, 10 days later, the wreck of the Titanic was finally located.

Following further dives, the expedition headed back to North America, where the Knorr docked on 9 September 1985. Amidst

MAIN
A portion of the first class C deck.

huge media interest, Ballard and his team held a press conference, concluding: 'It is quiet and peaceful and a fitting place for the remains of this greatest of sea tragedies to rest. May it forever remain that way and may God bless these found souls.'

The discovery of the wreck permitted a number of pieces in the Titanic story to be gradually pieced together. For example, the imagery recorded by the Argo's camera showed conclusively that the Titanic had broken up prior to sinking with the bow and stern sections separated by a distance of some 650 yards and with a considerable debris field surrounding it. Although the non-ferrous items on the ship were reasonably well preserved, all organic material – including bodies – had disappeared and the iron was incrusted with rust. The state of the ship and the depth at which she lay precluded any possibility of the wreck being raised.

Once the Titanic had been discovered, it was inevitable that interest in the ship would increase dramatically. Further exploration of the site has followed and, with advances in underwater photography and filming, stunning images of the wreck have emerged. Amongst the records produced from these trips is a stunning IMAX film, directed by James Cameron (who also directed the feature film Titanic with Kate Winslet and Leonardo di Caprio), which included remarkable footage of the ship's interior. Apart from the scientific interest, there have been a number of attempts to claim the salvage rights to the supposed treasure on board the ship and ownership has been subject to legal dispute on both sides of the Atlantic. There has also been legislation to try and ensure that the site of the wreck is – like those of warships sunk in battle – treated as a grave for those who perished. A number of items from the ship's

Chapter Fifteen

debris field have, however, been salvaged and placed on display. These items include unbroken pieces of crockery, taps, portholes and much else. Many of these artefacts were brought together for an exhibition at the National Maritime Museum, in Greenwich, during 1994 and 1995. Although the planning of the exhibition was not without controversy – largely as a result of concerns about material raised from an internationally recognised grave – it proved to be the most successful then held at the Museum.

The raising of material from the seabed is but one problem; after many years submerged to a depth of some two and a half miles and subjected, as a result to vast pressure, as well as to the impact of corrosion and chemical action, all the items recovered need to be carefully conserved prior to display.

Of course, whilst the individual items recovered from the Titanic can be treated by experts on shore, the greatest relic of them all – the remains of the ship itself – are much more vulnerable. The discovery of the ship and the subsequent voyages by remote cameras and, more recently by submersibles capable of taking people down to the wreck, as well as efforts to try and salvage parts from the debris field and ship itself have accelerated the process of the ship's own disintegration. The threat was recognised by Robert Ballard himself when he wrote in his book *The Discovery of the Titanic* (published in 1987): 'For now the greatest threat to the Titanic clearly comes from man, in the form of crude dredging operations.'

MAIN
A telegraph wheel from the Titanic.

Chapter Sixteen

The Titanic Myths

Almost from the point at which the ship sank, the Titanic has been the subject of various conspiracy theories and supposed curses. Amongst the various myths and legends that have sprung up over the years are the following (the majority of which are completely fallacious):

• That several Catholic workers at Harland & Wolff – a company noted historically for its strong bias towards Protestant employees – walked out as a result of anti-Catholic slogans painted on board; this graffiti was noted by crew members at Queenstown. One of the Catholics who walked off was alleged to have said 'This ship will not finish its first voyage.'

• That the construction of the ship was so rapid that at least one worker was sealed up in the hull and left to die. In fact, the number of casualties during the construction of the Titanic was lower than the one per £100,000 value of the contract that was the accepted norm at the time; only two fatalities are known to have occurred during the construction of the ship.

• That the reason the ship was given hull number 390904 is that, when shown in a mirror, '390904' can be read as 'No Popery'.

• That a cursed Egyptian mummy, nicknamed 'Shipwrecker', was on board, and that, in order to exact revenge on its owner, it inspired the sinking of the ship. There is, however, no record of the supposed mummy in the manifest of cargo taken on board the ship. The origin of the story may well have been the narration over dinner by the journalist William Stead – a noted spiritualist (as were many influential people at the time including the creator of Sherlock Holmes, Sir Arthur Conan Doyle) – of a mummy then on display in the British Museum (where it still remains).

• That the bottle of champagne used when the ship was christened at launching failed to break. Believed to be an indication of bad luck, this was unlikely to have happened with the Titanic as normal White Star Line policy was not to christen its ships when they were launched.

• That the notoriously parochial Aberdeen *Press and Journal* recorded the sinking under the headline 'Aberdeenshire Man Drowned at Sea'. The actual headline used was 'Mid-Atlantic Disaster: Titanic Sunk by Iceberg'. There were several other variations on this theme; all are equally fanciful.

• That there was a mystery ship present close to the Titanic; Joseph Boxhall believed that he'd seen the lights of a second vessel shortly after midnight and other members of the crew subsequently reported seeing lights as well. In addition, Colonel Gracie and other passengers also believed that they saw a second ship's lights. At the subsequent British inquiry, this vessel was identified as the Californian and thus led to considerable opprobrium being heaped on Captain Lord. Subsequent inquiries, particularly since the discovery of the wreck, have cast some doubt on this although the official position remains equivocal about the actual position of the Californian in relation to the actual sinking.

• That a large number of prominent passengers cancelled at the last moment with premonitions of disaster. A certain number undoubtedly did cancel but most of these were for more prosaic reasons. An American steel baron, Henry Clay Frick and his wife were booked to travel; however, Mrs Frick sprained her ankle whilst on Madeira; their booking was taken over by John Pierpoint Morgan, but he was forced to cancel as a result of over-running business negotiations. This ill-fated booking was then taken over by another American businessman, J Horace Harding, who eventually transferred to the Mauretania. The ex-US ambassador to France, Robert Bacon, was also scheduled to travel on the Titanic with his wife; however, the delayed arrival of his successor meant that he had to remain in France until after the ship had sailed. George Vanderbilt and his wife did cancel at the last minute, but this was more to do with his mother-in-law's dislike of maiden voyages (Vanderbilt's servant, Frederick Wheeler, did travel on the ship as a second class passenger, and was to die in the tragedy). In all some 55 bookings

were cancelled. There was, however, at least one premonition: a Mr and Mrs E W Bill from Philadelphia transferred to the Celtic as a result of a dream Mrs Bill had whilst staying in a London hotel shortly before their departure. There was an added complication in the travel plans of many potential passengers and that was that Britain was in the midst of a coal strike and White Star Line had been forced to try and obtain coal from a variety of sources; lack of coal meant that a number of other services were cancelled or delayed with inevitable confusion for potential passengers.

• That the Titanic and Olympic were switched during the second occasion when both were in dry-dock in Belfast, following the loss of the Olympic's propeller. The argument here is that, as a result of the Olympic's collision with HMS Hawke,

LEFT
Henry Clay Frick.

RIGHT
The Titanic in dry-dock Belfast..

the condition of the White Star liner was much worse than generally accepted and that, as a result, the company would find it difficult to obtain insurance cover for the ship. Therefore, the switch was arranged so that the compromised Olympic would sail as the brand new, and therefore easily insured, Titanic, so that when insurance assessors came to look at the Olympic (ex-Titanic), they would see a ship for which insurance could easily be given.

Chapter Seventeen

The Titanic in Popular Culture

BELOW
A postage stamp celebrating the release of the film *Titanic*.

The first books to feature the sinking of the Titanic – written by Lawrence Beesley and Archibald Gracie – appeared within months of the ship's demise and the first film, that written and starring Dorothy Gibson, also appeared during 1912. Since then a great deal about the ship has appeared in both fact and fiction.

Films about the Titanic include the following:

• *Saved from the Titanic* – The original silent film made in 1912 and starring Dorothy Gibson. This was a hugely successful film when released in May 1912 with prints being sent to the UK and France as well as being distributed in the USA. Unfortunately, despite this early success, there is no known print of this film in existence and it is therefore considered to be 'lost'. It's widely regarded as one of the greatest missing films of the silent era. Of all the films made by Dorothy Gibson, only one is known to survive and that is *The Lucky Holdup* (1912) that was located and rescued in 2001.

• *A Night to Remember* – Released in 1958, this was based on Walter Lord's bestselling book of the same name, which had been published three years earlier. Directed by Roy Baker and with a screenplay

by the noted thriller writer Eric Ambler, the film's stars included Kenneth More, David McCallum and Honor Blackman. Much of the film was shot at Pinewood Studios with the scenes in the water filmed at the nearby Ruislip Lido.

• *Raise the Titanic!* – Sir Lew Grade's multi-million pound epic was released in 1980. Based on the novel of the same name by Clive Cussler, the film was directed by

33 USA

A JAMES CAMERON FILM

TITANIC

Blockbuster Film

The Titanic in Popular Culture

BELOW
Actors prepare to film a lifeboat scene in the movie *A Night to Remember*.

Jerry Jameson and the cast included Jason Robards and Sir Alec Guinness. The plot revolved around the alleged presence on board the ship of 'byzanium', a material that is required to power a defence project. The highpoint of another lacklustre film is the point at which the liner suddenly re-emerges above the waterline. Commenting on the cost of the film, Grade stated that it would probably have been cheaper to have lowered the Atlantic.

• *Titanic* – Released in 1997 and starring Leonardo di Caprio and Kate Winslet, this James Cameron directed film is the highest

grossing film in the history of film-making. The film cost $200 million to make and ended up winning 11 Academy Awards.

• *Ghosts of the Abyss* – A stunning 3-D IMAX documentary filmed by James Cameron and released in 2003. The film was shot using specially created cameras, Jake and Elwood, to get closer to the wreck than ever before and actually to traverse the interior of the ship itself. Using CGI technology, the film also recreates how the ship looked when new. Cameron was joined in the filming and narration by the actor Bill Paxton, who played the role of Brock Lovett (a fictional character) in Cameron's 1997 blockbuster.

In terms of books, there has been a large number produced over the years. The first books to appear were those compiled by Lawrence Beesley – *The Loss of the SS* Titanic – and by Archibald Gracie – *The Truth about the* Titanic. Also published shortly after the actual tragedy were the official reports of both the British and US inquiries. It was in 1956 that the classic account, written by Walter Lord, *A Night to Remember* was first released and, with the discovery of the wreck itself, the number of books produced has grown significantly. A number of these – such as Dr Robert Ballard's *The Discovery of the* Titanic – include images taken of the

BELOW
Action scene from
the 1997 film *Titanic*.

RIGHT
Director James
Cameron answers
questions from an
audience at the book
signing for *Ghosts of
the Abyss.*

**RIGHT
BELOW**
Titanic artifacts from
the wreck.

wreck site itself. More recent books, such *Titanic: Destination Disaster – The Legends and the Reality –* also now include photographs of some of the artefacts recovered from the site. There are also a number of books devoted to the conspiracy theory, most notably *The Riddle of the Titanic* by Robin Gardiner and Dan van der Vat and Robin Gardiner's *Titanic: The Ship that Never Sank?*

As might also be expected, in an age of the internet, there are also countless web-sites devoted to the subject. The most comprehensive is perhaps www.encyclopedia-titanica.org. This site includes information on all passengers and crew members, identifying those who survived and those who died, along with potted biographies. Also included is a vast array of references to other sources, a search facility and a message board.

RMS Titanic Inc

Once the wreck was discovered there was a considerable debate as to actual ownership of the wreck and of the artefacts on board. Following legal action in the USA, RMS Titanic Inc, a subsidiary of Premier Exhibitions Inc, was granted salvor-in-possession rights to the ship by a US Federal Court in 1994, a decision that was confirmed by a second ruling in 1996. The company has undertaken seven expeditions – in 1987, 1993, 1994, 1996, 1998, 2000 and 2004 – to recover artefacts from the ship and, to date has raised some 5,500 objects in all. The artefacts raised include a 17-ton section of the actual bow section to a child's marble. These artefacts, along with documentation, form the basis of a travelling exhibition – Titanic: The Artefact Exhibition – that has been seen by some 15 million people over the past decade.

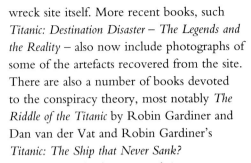

Chapter Eighteen

Titanic in Retrospect

RIGHT
Artifacts from the Titanic on display.

BELOW
Millvina Dean, Britain's only remaining Titanic survivor, now aged 96.

As the centenary of the sinking of the Titanic approaches in 2012, the story will pass from living history to true history as the final survivors die – there is only one alive at the time of writing – and those who were alive at the time are sadly reduced, what will remain of the Titanic?

There will be the physical monuments constructed to those who lost their lives in the sinking. These include the statue raised to Wallace Hartley in Colne, Lancashire, the 'below decks, memorial now located at Holy Rood Church, Southampton, the monument raised to the ship's engineers dedicated in 1914 in the public gardens in Southampton, and the memorial constructed near Belfast City Hall, not far from where the ship was built.

There will be the various artefacts that have been brought to the surface and some of which will feature in the future in the new museum under development in Belfast, the centrepiece of which will be the tender Nomadic repatriated from France.

There will be the wreck itself, although the continuing deterioration of the remains and the degradation of the site caused by the presence of human activity over the past 20 years means that the wreck itself will gradually be lost forever.

There are the countless photographs – some taken whilst the ship was afloat, others since the wreck was rediscovered – that will provide a constant reminder of the splendour of the ship itself. There are also the representations, in fact and in fiction, in film and in books that will entertain and educate.

And there is the myth: the tragic story of a ship believed to be unsinkable that was lost with more than 1,500 lives on a cold April night in 1912.

Also available:

Our best-selling *Focus On* range.

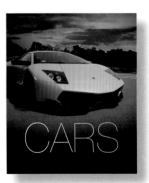

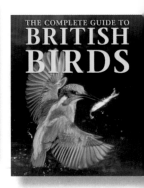

Our fact-packed *Picture This* range.

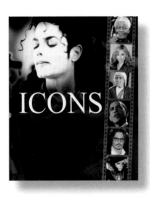
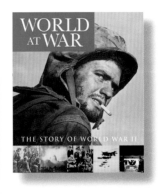
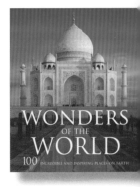